Sachie's Kitchen

SACHIE NOMURA

HarperCollins*Publishers*

THIS BOOK IS DEDICATED
TO MY FAMILY

CONTENTS

INTRODUCTION

Konnichiwa and hello! My name is Sachie Nomura, and it is amazing to me that I'm typing the introduction to my first ever book. This is a treasured collection of some of the most popular recipes and dishes from my culture, my award-winning cooking school, Sachie's Kitchen, and my TV show of the same name.

I was born and grew up in Hekinan city, in Japan's Aichi prefecture, famous for being the home of Toyota.

I have always loved food. My mum and aunty were keen foodies and I started to cook when I was seven. Both my parents were extremely busy, working full-time (my mum had her own business and my dad worked for Toyota), so I was forced to become self-sufficient and also make sure my younger brother was fed. I would do the prep work as a kitchen hand for my mum when she came home from work and then she would cook the meals (with me watching). This evolved to waitressing at local restaurants, which helped me understand how important great food plus good service is in creating a total experience.

When I was 17, I had to decide whether to go to university or work – so, a lot of pressure. One day during the winter holidays, my mum suggested perhaps I could go overseas to study English. That was the planting of the travel seed. I planned to go to the USA, but I met a friend's friend who had just returned from studying in Palmerston North and he told me all about New Zealand. (I must confess that, before this, I didn't entirely know where New Zealand was – all I knew was that it was home to sheep. Lots and lots of sheep.) He told me that the New Zealanders

are very friendly, the climate is similar to Japan and it is very safe with no guns! So, I came to study English first, then majored in Chinese and Linguistics at Auckland University and met my Malaysian Chinese husband.

I worked in a local travel agency and a hotel, but as my culinary skills grew I was fortunate to live with and be home-schooled by some of the leading Japanese chefs in Auckland, who would rotate in and out on overseas exchanges for about a decade. There was a long period of time when these chefs all lived close by to each other, in the same streets or in close suburbs in Auckland, and I happened to flat or live close to them. After 10 hours working in the heat of the kitchen many of them wouldn't want to cook again at home, so I learnt all my skills informally under their tutelage, kind of as their private chef! This was invaluable experience. I learnt a variety of different techniques, and particularly how to be creative in the home using domestic appliances and ingredients.

One day in late 2009 I was shocked by the news that two of my colleague's friends had died from sudden heart attacks. In my head I could hear my mum's voice telling me as a child that 'If there is something that you really want to do, you should give it a good shot, so there are no regrets in life.' That day I went home, spoke to my husband, locked myself in our spare room, took out a pencil and drew a mind map of the things I wanted to achieve in life. I knew I wanted to use my knowledge of Japanese cooking and my passion for Asian expression. I have lived almost exactly half my life in Asia and half in my adopted home of New Zealand. My brainstorming turned into the vision for Sachie's Kitchen and that original scribbled business plan is now framed on the wall of the cooking school.

My husband said he would give me a year to build my business. I felt very strongly about it, so I left my job in the middle of the worst recession in 30 years, did a lot of market research, spoke to many people and began my journey. I took a loan from my husband, constructed six kitchens and, after an eight-month fit-out, I opened the doors of my dream.

I was booked up two months in advance and I paid my husband back a year later. I'm really proud that my business provides employment to passionate immigrants, is completely debt-free and absolutely thriving. Sachie's Kitchen has become the largest and most awarded Asian cooking school in Australasia. More than 5500 happy cooks have come through the school and we run one to two classes a day, six days a week.

Photo by Laura Zhao

MY STYLE IS ABOUT PASSING ON COOKING SKILLS AND ASIAN RECIPES THAT ARE EASY FOR YOU TO TAKE HOME. I USE DOMESTIC APPLIANCES AND ACCESSIBLE INGREDIENTS.
AND MY GOAL IS SIMPLY TO INSPIRE PEOPLE TO EAT MORE INTERESTING FOOD.

As the team has grown into a mini United Nations, we now offer more than just Japanese – Thai, Vietnamese, Indian, Malaysian and Chinese classes are all available; the full spectrum of Asian food expression.

It all seems like a fairy tale. Through the cooking school and a few chance opportunities, I was asked to write columns for a national newspaper, speak on national radio and then front my own primetime TV show, *Sachie's Kitchen*.

I don't like to call myself a chef and I have always asked the staff in my cooking school not to call me that. My style is about passing on cooking skills and Asian recipes that are easy for you to take home. I use domestic appliances and accessible ingredients, and my goal is simply to inspire people to eat more interesting food. Hopefully, with these recipes you can experience real Asian food culture.

It is my passion and honour to be able to share with you the recipes that come from our heart, the 'kokoro' that is woven through everything we do at Sachie's Kitchen. I hope you try these recipes and share them with your friends and family, because if you do that, then I will have achieved my life's mission.

Doumo arigato gozaimasu!
Thank you.
Sachie

INGREDIENTS
IN SACHIE'S KITCHEN

1. BONITO FLAKES (KATSUOBUSHI)
Katsuobushi are shaved, dried bonito (tuna) flakes, used to make dashi stock or as a garnish for dishes such as okonomiyaki (Japanese savoury pancake).

2. BUCKWHEAT/SOBA NOODLES
Made from wheat flour, buckwheat flour, salt and water, these thin grey noodles have a distinctively earthy taste. Please note that 100 per cent buckwheat noodles are gluten-free and are available in some stores. Other varieties of soba such as green tea- or plum-flavoured noodles are often available.

3. BURDOCK (GOBOU)
This root vegetable is rich in dietary fibre, low in calories and was historically used as a natural remedy for treating indigestion and skin conditions, among other things. Scrub the skin off lightly with a sponge or the back of a knife rather than peeling it off. If you want to avoid discoloration, soak in water before using, but not for too long or you will lose nutritional value. Great for stir-fries, stews, salads or in soups.

4. COOKING SAKE (RYORISHU)
This sake is for cooking and not for drinking!

When we use sake for seasoning, it serves to tenderise meat and seafood. It also helps bring out the umami ('fifth flavour' or 'pleasant savoury taste') in each ingredient.

5. DAIKON
This versatile white root vegetable is also known as Chinese radish and has a digestive effect. Peel off the skin before using. Daikon has a multitude of uses, but some ideas are to grate and serve with tempura; shred and add to your salad or sashimi plate; or cut into chunks and add to your stew, soup or hotpot.

6. DASHI
A Japanese stock made from either fish, seaweed or mushrooms. You can make the stock from scratch, but people often use a powdered version at home. The common types of dashi are katsuo (tuna/bonito), niboshi (dried sardines) and konbu (kelp).

7. DRIED SHIITAKE MUSHROOMS
These are distinctive by their dark brown colour, meaty texture and intense flavour, compared to fresh shiitakes. Soak in warm water for 15–20 minutes before using. The soaking liquid can be used for soup stock.

8. EDAMAME BEANS

These green soy beans, often found in the frozen section in your local supermarket, are a great alternative to junk food like chips. Defrost and serve as nibbles or use to make soup or dipping sauce.

9. GARLIC CHIVES (NIRA)

A type of chive with flat leaves and a garlic taste. Great for stir-fries and hotpots, and when chopped and added to your dumpling fillings.

10. GLUTINOUS RICE FLOUR

A white flour derived from glutinous rice and used to make mochi (sticky rice cakes), steamed buns and many other dishes.

11. GOCHUJANG

Korea's traditional fermented condiment is a deep red, hot chilli paste made from red chilli, rice or barley, soy beans and salt. It gives a rich spiciness to a dish. Use a small amount to start until you get used to the heat.

12. JAPANESE MAYONNAISE

This is one of my favourite sauces and many Westerners know it affectionately as yum-yum sauce! Great in salads and as a dipping sauce.

13. JAPANESE MUSTARD

Karashi means mustard in Japanese. Often we call Japanese mustard 'Wa garashi' and Western mustard 'Yo garashi'. Wa garashi is available as a yellow paste or powder – add lukewarm water to the powder to make a paste. Wa garashi is sharper and stronger in flavour and taste. If you can't find Wa garashi, use American mustard.

14. KIMCHI

A traditional Korean side dish, often served as fermented Chinese cabbage, carrots, spring onion and radish in chilli paste with other condiments.

Very strong in taste; sour and spicy. Eat this as a side dish, or add to a hotpot or okonomiyaki (Japanese pancake) to add spiciness.

15. KONBU

This dried sea kelp is often used to make soup stock. It comes in dry form, so wipe with a damp cloth before using.

16. LA-YU (JAPANESE CHILLI OIL)

Add a few drops to dumpling dipping sauce to give some heat and kick to the dish.

17. LOTUS ROOT (RENKON)

The root of the lotus plant has many holes inside, a crunchy texture and is mild in flavour. Often found in the frozen section of Asian grocery stores. Add vinegar to water and soak the lotus root before using to avoid discoloration. Slice to stir-fry, or deep-fry to make renkon chips.

18. MATCHA

A type of green tea that comes in very fine powder form, this is used to make matcha tea (Japanese traditional tea) and is different from regular green tea. Great for colouring and often used to add a light green-tea flavour to iconic Japanese desserts such as green tea ice cream, green tea cheesecakes and mochi (rice cakes).

19. MIRIN

This sweet cooking wine has a golden colour and is made from rice or glutinous rice. It not only adds a mild sweetness to the ingredients and gives gloss or shine to the dish, but it also has the great effect of reducing unpleasant smells from meat or seafood. An essential condiment for making delicious teriyaki chicken.

20. MISO

Fermented soy bean paste made from soy bean, rice or barley, salt and water. The taste, colour and texture vary from region to region in Japan. The

24

21

25

20

27 23 29

29

29

22

28 26

30

main types are white miso (shiro miso) and red miso (aka miso) and mixed miso (awase miso). White miso has a light brown/ivory colour, a mild flavour and sweet taste. Red miso is dark brown with a rich and strong salty taste. Miso is not only used for the well-known miso soup, but is also fantastic in marinades for meat or fish.

21. NORI
A type of seaweed that comes in dark green/black sheets. Nori is used to make sushi rolls and rice balls, and can also be shredded or bought in powdered form (this is called 'aonori') and sprinkled over your favourite dishes to add a unique texture. Aonori is particularly used in okonomiyaki (Japanese pancake). If nori sheets have softened from oxidisation, don't throw them away ... Flip them a couple of times over an open flame and this will immediately bring back crunchiness.

22. PANKO (JAPANESE BREADCRUMBS)
Used to deep-fry vegetables, seafood and meat and give a crunchy texture to dishes. Also used in meatballs/patties as a combining agent.

23. POTATO STARCH (KATAKURIKO)
This is mainly used as a thickening agent for dishes or used for deep-frying. For a thickening agent, dissolve in a little water first and pour into the pan just before finishing the dish.

24. RAMEN NOODLES
Ramen dough is made from wheat flour, salt, water and kansui (alkaline mineral water) to create a unique texture, taste and colour that has made the noodle iconic. Somewhat like pasta in Italy, ramen comes in different shapes: thin, thick, straight or wavy.

25. RED BEAN PASTE (ANKO)
Sweet red bean paste made from azuki beans and sugar. Often used to make desserts in Japan.

26. RICE VINEGAR
Made from rice and distinguished by its pale yellow colour, this is mild in flavour and is not as acidic as Western vinegar. Suitable for making sushi vinegar and pickles.

27. SHICHIMI
This is also called 'Japanese seven chillies'. Depending on the brand, the majority of shichimi is made from seven different Japanese spices – any combination of red chilli pepper, sansho (Japanese pepper), rapeseed, black sesame seeds, sesame seeds, shiso (perilla leaves), hemp seed, ground ginger and nori. It is used as a condiment for noodle soups or dipping sauce.

28. SESAME OIL
A very popular oil in Asia that is often used for stir-frying, making dressings or dripped into noodle soup just before serving to add a unique sesame flavour.

29. SESAME SEEDS/BLACK SESAME SEEDS (GOMA/KUROGOMA)
I recommend buying toasted sesame seeds. Otherwise, toast before use in a frying pan over medium heat but be careful not to burn. Use as a garnish or grind the seeds to make a powder or paste.

30. SOY SAUCE
This is the most common condiment used in Japanese cuisine and is made by fermentation of soy beans, wheat and salt. Dark soy sauce (koikuchi) and light soy sauce (usukuchi) are commonly used – light soy sauce is paler in colour but actually has a slightly saltier taste.

31. SURIMI (CRAB STICK)
Surimi is mainly made from ground fish flesh with additives such as salt, sugar and food colouring. It comes in different shapes and forms, but the most common one is mimic crab meat. This has a slightly sweet flavour, which is perfect for mixing with mayonnaise for sushi or salad.

32. SUSHI GINGER (GARI)
This is young ginger that has been pickled in sugar, vinegar and salt. Often used as a garnish for sushi and sashimi, to cleanse your palate.

33. TOFU
Bean curd made by coagulating soy bean milk and forming into a block. Silken/soft (kimugoshi) tofu is suitable for salads, soups or eating by itself with just a drip of soy sauce and bonito flakes. Firm (momen) tofu is most suitable for dishes such as hotpot.

34. UDON NOODLES
Made from wheat flour, salt and water, these noodles are characterised by their white colour and thick, chewy texture.

35. WAKAME
Another form of seaweed, often used in miso soup, noodle soups and salad. Wakame comes in dry form, so either soak in water to soften before using or add a few pieces to soup. Be careful not to use too much, as the pieces expand greatly in size.

36. WASABI
This Japanese horseradish tastes very peppery and pungent. Fresh wasabi root is very expensive and not readily available, hence wasabi is often seen in powder or paste form. If you are using wasabi powder, add water to make a paste. Use a little powder to start as you will feel it through your nose if you use too much!

TARTARE SAUCE
(PAGE 158)

WAFU DRESSING
(PAGE 54)

TEMPURA SAUCE
(PAGE 150)

TUNA TATAKI DRESSING
(PAGE 51)

SESAME SEED DRESSING
(PAGE 68)

ONION DRESSING
(PAGE 56)

PONZU SAUCE
(PAGE 146)

SUSHI ZU
(PAGE 118)

SWEET MISO SAUCE
(PAGE 162)

SESAME SEED PASTE
(PAGE 60)

ESSENTIAL UTENSILS

1. KNIVES

Knives are the ultimate tool in any chef's or foodie's kitbag – a question I am often asked in the cooking school is what country makes the best knife? Germany, Switzerland? Well I am understandably very biased – but it's well-recognised that Japan makes the best knives in the world, with proud tradition and roots steeped in the ancient techniques of Samurai sword-making.

Japanese steel is renowned for updating ancient forging skills with state-of-the-art manufacturing and technology, so the knives are famed throughout the world. An interesting fact is that many of the surgical scalpels you see in the hands of surgeons are from the Seki prefecture in Japan!

There are several distinct differences between Japanese and European knives. Japanese knives tend to be lighter because most are stamped, not forged. They also typically have little or no bolster, and the edges are sharpened more steeply. There are actually a large number of different types of Japanese kitchen knives. The most commonly used types in the Japanese kitchen are the deba bocho (filleting knife), the santoku bocho (all-purpose utility knife) and the nagiri (Japanese vegetable knife).

My knife of choice is the nagiri – it is great for dicing, mincing and making julienne. The flat edge makes it very easy to get consistent cuts. Though it may look like a cleaver, the way it is used is completely different. Instead of hacking away, you use a forward-thrusting motion, where the edge stays parallel to the cutting surface.

One of the episodes of the TV show had me visit a 16th-generation knife craftsman, and when I returned from Osaka, I came back with an even greater respect for my knives, which I hadn't thought was possible. The old master, who has specialised in the process of sharpening knives for over 50 years, said to me that there is actually a sixth element to taste in addition to sweet, sour, bitter, salty and umami. He remarked to me that there exists literally a 'taste of sharpness of knife'. At first, I wasn't sure what he meant, and he explained that 'If your knife is sharp, then you won't damage the flesh of the fish, meat or vegetable. When you cook, the taste goes deeper into the ingredients; when you eat a slice of sashimi cut by an artisan blade, it will be smooth and melt in your mouth in a different way to flesh that has been cut by a blunt blade, as it hasn't been damaged.'

While he was recounting this story to me, he paused and checked the sharpness of the blade by shaving his arm hair. I noticed he was almost bald! It was an honour to experience and witness the master's attention and devotion to his art, and it left me inspired and with a feeling of deep responsibility that I must share this dying craft with the rest of the world. All I can simply suggest is, if you get a chance to purchase an authentic Japanese knife, do so – you and your food won't ever regret it.

2. RICE COOKER

This is the only appliance that was never switched off in my house when I was a child. I'm guessing it's because my brother, Shuhei, was a notorious early-riser (unlike me – I still hate getting up in the morning) and, as a growing boy, hungry all the time. Shuhei would just make himself a simple bowl of rice and some pickles for his breakfast, and I'd wake up to find him sitting in front of the TV.

3. CHOPSTICKS

I don't think there is any Asian kitchen utensil more iconic than chopsticks. Amazingly, approximately one-third of the world's population use chopsticks, so it may be more useful than you think to know the fascinating etiquette attached to this ancient tradition. In Japan there are two different types of chopsticks. The one that you often see in restaurants is called 'hashi' and the other is called 'sai bashi', which

are cooking chopsticks. The difference between the two is that cooking chopsticks are a lot longer than the normal ones and I often use these for a huge variety of kitchen purposes that otherwise require multiple utensils. This saves a lot of space and helps with organisation. I use them for activities such as beating eggs, stir-frying foods, deep-frying tempura, helping with presentation such as putting garnish on the plates – it becomes your one-stop, multi-purpose tool!

I actually don't remember how or when I learnt to use chopsticks. I think it's a rite of passage for every Asian child, otherwise you'll be left to starve, so I must have learnt at home from my parents or at school. I'm not quite at the skill level where I can catch flies with my chopsticks like my husband tries to do (and fails, mind you), but it's an important part of the Asian culture, and if you want to get around Asia it's highly advisable you practise!

In Japanese culture, there is actually quite an etiquette around chopsticks:

- Don't ever hold the same object with two people's chopsticks i.e. pass food around from chopstick to chopstick – it doesn't matter if you are close friends, lovers or husband and wife! (This is extremely taboo as this only happens during a funeral when collecting the bones after the bodies have been cremated.)

- Take care not to stab your chopsticks into your food, particularly upright into your bowl of rice, as it signifies dead person's food.

- Don't move your plate with your chopsticks.

- Whatever you touch with your chopsticks is considered yours, so digging through the plate or bowl of food looking to select what cut of meat or vegetable you'd like would be considered quite rude. You should also avoid licking or sucking your chopsticks. Also putting food back after picking it up with your chopsticks will imply that you don't appreciate the food, so avoid this too.

One habit that I was taught by my elders when I was young was to always leave my chopsticks resting on the chopstick case whenever we would go to a restaurant. I was also instructed that we should never place our chopsticks on the tabletop, unless you have finished your meal. To this day, I always leave the eating edge of the chopsticks on the side of my plate or with the chopstick resting on the case or on a little stand called a 'hashioki'.

4. MORTAR AND PESTLE
The humble mortar and pestle is an essential kitchen utensil and is very common in Asian pantries – whether they be Japanese, Thai, Vietnamese or Indian! The Japanese version is called a 'suribachi' (meaning 'grinding bowl') and has its own variation from other Asian cultures.

The main reason is because Japanese cuisine comparatively doesn't use as many spices (such as Indian spices) or herbs in the cooking that many Southeast Asian people use. We mainly use our mortar and pestle for grinding sesame seeds and nuts for things such as black sesame seed paste, walnut paste with miso, etc. Hence, you see the grooves that are created on the inside of the mortar.

My mum has a super-large one at home and she often places it in between her feet while she grinds seeds, for stability. I have fond memories from when I used to complain to my mum about having to use the mortar and pestle when I was young as my arms were too weak and got tired very quickly. Now I can't imagine not using it!

Tip: If you don't have a Japanese or a normal mortar and pestle, you can use a spice grinder to grind seeds.

5. OTOSHIBUTA
Otoshibuta (meaning 'drop lid') is one of the cooking tools that we use all the time when we are cooking stews or braising fish, meat or vegetables. The otoshibuta is placed inside of the cooking pot, on top of the food, with the lid placed on top, i.e. it acts as a double lid. The purpose is to help circulate the liquid beneath the otoshibuta with the outcome of creating an evenness of taste through the food.

An otoshibuta is normally made of wood. However, a tip – if you can't find an otoshibuta, you can substitute either baking paper or tin foil cut to fit inside of the pot. As baking paper and tin foil are light in weight, please make sure to cut a little hole in the middle – this will prevent bubbles from forming underneath and pushing the baking paper or tin foil too far upwards. (For step-by-step images, see page 94.)

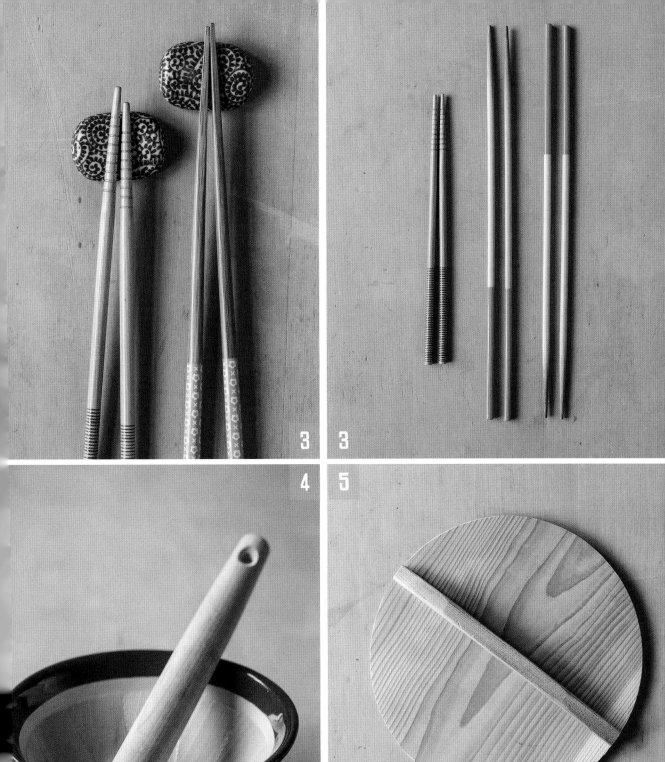

3

3

4

5

七転び'八起き

NANA KOROBI, YAOKI

Meaning: Fall seven times, stand eight.
(That is, never give up.)

I am constantly amazed that in such a short sentence, there is such guidance on how to live one's life strongly. It's almost impossible to argue with the truths in proverbs that have been passed down from our ancestors.

Whenever I felt stuck or felt like a failure, my parents would quote this saying to encourage me to try again!

SIDES TO SHARE

In my home and cooking school, we say 'sharing is caring', and certainly this applies to how we eat as well. If you come to eat with my family, you will see at least four to five side dishes and one main dish. Everything is served at once on our dining table and everyone digs in at the same time!

A tip: I love to cook big portions for mains and keep the leftovers to serve as a side dish the next day, so I don't always have to cook five or six dishes per meal. Having pickles in the fridge is great too – they last for a long time and I like to regularly serve them as a side dish and palate cleanser.

My suggestion would be to choose two dishes from this chapter and add one more dish from 'Mains' to complete your Japanese meal!

ピクルス

CUCUMBER AND CELERY PICKLES

SERVES
4

PREPARATION TIME
7 minutes plus 1 hour
marinating

COOKING TIME
nil

INGREDIENTS
¼ telegraph cucumber,
  seeds removed
1 celery stalk
2 dried chillies, chopped
200ml sushi vinegar (use
  ready-made or see recipe
  on page 118)

There are a number of different pickle recipes in Japan and some can take up to a month to make! This takes only seven minutes to prepare. I love it because the recipe is nice and simple and the pickle adds a lovely tangy, spicy flavour to anything you serve.

METHOD
Cut all vegetables into bite-sized chunks and place in a 2-cup (500ml) glass jar.

Add chopped chilli to jar. Pour in vinegar and put lid on jar.

Keep in fridge for 1 hour, and drain vinegar away before serving.

なますと白菜の漬け物

NAMASU AND HAKUSAI PICKLES

SERVES
4

PREPARATION TIME
10 minutes plus 30 minutes marinating

COOKING TIME
nil

NAMASU
½ daikon, shredded
1 small carrot, shredded
2 Tbsp sea salt
¼ cup sugar
¼ cup rice vinegar
lime zest, optional
chilli flakes, optional

HAKUSAI
¼ Chinese cabbage, chopped into small pieces
1 Tbsp konbu
2 dried chillies, chopped
2 tsp sea salt

There are a number of methods for preserving food in Japan, and pickling is a way to enjoy our seasonal vegetables all year round. Namasu has a sweet and sour flavour, while hakusai pickle is more salty. I like to serve these as condiments with other dishes or as palate cleansers. Both will keep in the fridge for up to a week.

NAMASU METHOD
Put daikon and carrot in a large bowl. Sprinkle with sea salt and massage by hand for a couple of minutes to remove all moisture.

Rinse daikon and carrot under cold water and squeeze out water.

Place daikon and carrot in a zip-lock bag with sugar and vinegar. If using, add lime zest and chilli flakes. Massage gently to dissolve sugar and leave in fridge for 30 minutes. Lightly squeeze out liquid before serving.

HAKUSAI METHOD
Put Chinese cabbage in a zip-lock bag. Add konbu, chilli and sea salt, and massage together for 1 minute. Leave in fridge for 30 minutes. Squeeze out liquid to serve.

枝豆とアボカドの冷やしスープ

MINTY EDAMAME AND AVOCADO COLD SOUP

SERVES
2

PREPARATION TIME
5 minutes

COOKING TIME
nil

INGREDIENTS
200g frozen edamame
  beans, defrosted and
  hulled
1 avocado
2 handfuls of mint leaves
1 tsp flaky sea salt
black pepper, to taste

This is a perfect soup to serve on a hot summer day. Serve chilled and enjoy the unique flavours of edamame and mint with a hint of avocado.

METHOD
Place edamame, avocado, mint and 2 cups (500ml) water in a food processor and mix until smooth (or use stick blender).

Season with the flaky sea salt and pepper. Serve cold.

豆腐とわかめのみそ汁
TOFU AND WAKAME MISO SOUP

In Japan, we have a bowl of rice and a bowl of miso soup at least once a day. To go for more than a couple of days without either would make me start to feel agitated! I use very basic ingredients for this soup, but you can add vegetables, meat or fish to make your own version.

METHOD

Bring 800ml water to the boil in a saucepan.

Reduce heat to medium, add dashi and tofu and cook for 1 minute.

Stir in miso until dissolved and add spring onion.

Place a pinch of dried wakame in each serving bowl and pour miso soup over the top.

SERVES
4

PREPARATION TIME
5 minutes

COOKING TIME
5 minutes

INGREDIENTS
½ tsp dashi powder
50g silken tofu, chopped
2 Tbsp white or mixed miso
1 spring onion, chopped
dried wakame

稲荷寿司

INARI SUSHI

MAKES
16–18 pieces

PREPARATION TIME
15 minutes

COOKING TIME
nil

INGREDIENTS

- 4 cups cooked white short- or medium-grain rice
- 4½ Tbsp sushi vinegar (use ready-made or see recipe on page 118)
- 6 Tbsp chopped sushi ginger
- 2 tsp black toasted sesame seeds
- 16–18 pieces inari (tofu bags)

This is a great pot luck or 'bring a plate' dish if you want to impress your friends. (They need never know that it doesn't take long to make!) Inari are great for lunch boxes, too – your kids will love you. The taste of the sushi ginger complements the sweetness of the tofu bags.

METHOD

Put warm rice in a large non-stainless steel bowl. Add sushi vinegar, sushi ginger and toasted sesame seeds, and mix well with a cutting action to prevent rice becoming mushy. Try to coat each rice grain.

Open inari bags gently and put 2 tablespoons rice in each one. Arrange, upside-down, on an attractive plate.

刺身の盛り合わせ

SASHIMI PLATE

SERVES
2–3

PREPARATION TIME
15–20 minutes

COOKING TIME
nil

In Japan, we love to eat raw seafood – our term for this is 'sashimi'. For a plate of sashimi, you will need sashimi-grade, very fresh raw fish. If you are unsure, befriend a keen fisherman, or simply ask the local fishmonger if their catch is fresh enough to eat as sashimi. Salmon, snapper, tarakihi, gurnard, John Dory and tuna are all lovely eaten raw.

INGREDIENTS

100g fillet sashimi-grade salmon, skin and bones removed

100g fillet sashimi-grade snapper, skin and bones removed

100g fillet sashimi-grade kingfish, skin and bones removed

1 tsp wasabi powder or ½ tsp wasabi paste

100g daikon, shredded

sushi ginger, to serve

soy sauce, to serve

METHOD

Holding your sharp knife at a 90° angle to the chopping board, slice the salmon into small block shapes.

Holding your knife at a 45° angle and cutting against the grain, slice the snapper towards the tail, as shown in the pictures (see pages 44–46).

If using wasabi powder, add ½ tsp water to make paste.

Place daikon on a plate, add sashimi and wasabi paste, and serve with sushi ginger and soy sauce.

1 2
3 4

5

6

7

8

9 10
11 12

残り物には福がある

NOKORIMONO NI WA
FUKU GA ARU

Meaning: Luck exists in the leftovers.
(That is, there is luck in the last helping.)

ビートルートと梅酒のサーモンマリネ
BEETROOT AND PLUM WINE SALMON

SERVES
3-4

PREPARATION TIME
10 minutes plus overnight marinating

COOKING TIME
nil

INGREDIENTS
450g fillet sashimi-grade salmon, skin and bones removed
½ beetroot, shredded
100ml plum wine
2 Tbsp flaky sea salt
1 lime, cut into half, to serve

When I visited the amazing salmon farms in beautiful Nelson, New Zealand, I was inspired by the taste and colour of this dish. Instead of the vodka and sugar of the original recipe, I've recreated this with Japanese plum wine, which gives it a totally unique flavour. Don't forget a squeeze of lime juice before you eat.

METHOD
Place whole salmon fillet in a zip-lock bag with beetroot, plum wine and sea salt. Marinate overnight in the fridge.

Slice salmon finely and serve with lime.

マグロのタタキ

TUNA TATAKI

I love the simple but elegant look of this dish and the taste of seared tuna. It's fantastic as a starter to impress dinner guests.

METHOD

Heat a frying pan to very high heat. Coat the block of tuna with sesame oil and place in pan. Sear each side for 10 seconds and set aside to cool.

To prepare garnish, soak spring onion in iced water for a couple of minutes until it curls. Drain and set aside.

To make dressing, bring sake and mirin to boil in a small pan and remove from heat to cool. Add soy sauce and lime juice and mix well.

Slice tuna into 5mm pieces and arrange on a serving plate. Garnish with spring onion and micro herbs. Drizzle with dressing and sprinkle with shichimi powder and lime zest.

SERVES
4

PREPARATION TIME
5 minutes

COOKING TIME
5 minutes

INGREDIENTS
400g block sashimi-grade tuna
1 Tbsp sesame oil

DRESSING
1 Tbsp sake
2 Tbsp mirin
2 Tbsp soy sauce
1 tsp lime juice

GARNISH
1 spring onion, white part only, cut into julienne
iced water
micro herbs
shichimi powder (Japanese seven chillies), or chilli powder, to taste
lime zest, to taste

ほうれん草の和え物

TUNA
WITH SPINACH

SERVES
2–3

PREPARATION TIME
5 minutes

COOKING TIME
1 minute

INGREDIENTS
450g Savoy spinach
185g tin tuna in oil
2 tsp soy sauce

It may sound slightly unusual to non-Japanese, but this is one of the dishes my mum always made for my lunch box or as a side dish for dinner when spinach was in season. It has the perfect combination: tasty, very economical and quick to prepare!

METHOD

Bring a pot of salted water to the boil. Add spinach by holding the leaves and dipping the stems into the hot water first. Hold the stems in for about 10 seconds, then push the leaves into the water and boil for 30–45 seconds until stems are softened. Refresh in cold water to prevent further cooking.

Squeeze water from spinach, cut into 4cm lengths and put in a bowl.

Drain tuna and add to spinach with soy sauce. Mix well and refrigerate until you serve.

牛のタタキサラダ

BEEF
TATAKI SALAD

SERVES
4

PREPARATION TIME
15 minutes

COOKING TIME
2–3 minutes

INGREDIENTS
1 x 280g beef sirloin or
　scotch fillet
iced water

WAFU DRESSING
3 Tbsp soy sauce
1 Tbsp cooking sake
2 tsp sugar
2 tsp mirin
50ml rice vinegar
juice of ¼ lemon
1 Tbsp grapeseed or salad oil
1 Tbsp sesame oil
¼ onion, grated
1 tsp sesame seeds
pinch of salt

SALAD
2 handfuls of shredded
　cabbage (red or green)

Tataki means 'pounded with a stick', but we also use this word to describe a style of cooking meat or fish – I often use beef fillet or tuna steaks. The meat is seared over very high heat, thinly sliced, and served with a variety of dressings or sauces, which makes this incredibly versatile as a starter, side dish or a main. Here I've served the meat as part of a salad.

METHOD

Heat a frying pan over very high heat. When very hot, cook steak for 30 seconds on both sides and then plunge steak into iced water for 30 seconds. Dry with paper towels.

Cut steak into 5mm slices, or thinner if you prefer.

Whisk together all dressing ingredients or put in a jam jar and shake well.

Arrange cabbage on plates and place sliced beef on top. Pour dressing over beef tataki and salad.

Japanese mayonnaise goes well with this dish too!

サーモンサラダとオニオンソース

SALMON SALAD WITH SPECIAL ONION DRESSING

SERVES
4

PREPARATION TIME
15 minutes

COOKING TIME
5 minutes

INGREDIENTS
150g cold smoked salmon
½ sunny (fancy) lettuce
¼ daikon, peeled and cut
   into julienne
handful of black olives
50g watercress
50g feta cheese, crumbled

DRESSING
½ red onion, chopped
2–3 Tbsp rice vinegar
2 Tbsp olive oil
1 Tbsp mirin
1 tsp brown sugar
½ tsp wasabi powder or
   paste
sea salt and black pepper,
   to taste

I love the extremely distinctive colour of this dressing. The secret is that it's derived from the red onion. There is also a spicy kick provided by the wasabi, but you can leave this out if you aren't a big fan.

METHOD
Arrange lettuce, daikon, olives, watercress and feta on a large plate.

To make dressing, put all ingredients in a food processor or use a stick blender and pulse until smooth. The colour will change to pink. (If you use brown onion, the dressing will be white.) Season with salt and pepper.

Arrange salmon on top of salad and drizzle with dressing.

Tip: If you can't find daikon, you can substitute carrots.

豆腐がんも

TOFU-GANMO

This is a journey to a new way of enjoying tofu, rather than simply adding it to miso soup or salad. This is one of our family's recipes and we call it 'ganmo' – deep-fried tofu. To add a distinctive taste and texture, we always add chopped squid.

METHOD

Place block of tofu between 2 dinner plates and leave for 30 minutes on bench top to remove moisture.

Squeeze water from shiitakes and chop very finely.

Place all ingredients except oil in a large bowl, season with salt and white pepper and mix well by hand. (The tofu will break up and become paste-like in the process.)

Heat oil to 180°C in a wok or saucepan. Scoop 1 tablespoon mixture and slide gently into the oil. Add 3 or 4 more scoops to the pan – be patient while the tofu is in oil and try not to touch it too much or it will break. Once the outside has started to cook, you can use chopsticks to move the tofu around. Deep-fry for 3–4 minutes until golden-brown.

Drain on paper towels and serve hot with grated ginger and soy sauce for dipping.

MAKES
15–20

PREPARATION TIME
15–20 minutes plus
30 minutes to drain tofu

COOKING TIME
10–15 minutes

INGREDIENTS
350g block firm tofu
3 dried shiitake mushrooms (about 20g), soaked in hot water for 10 minutes
½ carrot, finely chopped
100g squid, chopped
1 egg
1 spring onion, chopped
3 Tbsp rice flour
1 tsp soy sauce
1 tsp dashi powder
canola or rice bran oil, for deep-frying
soy sauce and grated ginger, to serve

胡麻和え
GOMA-AE
WITH BEANS

SERVES
4

PREPARATION TIME
5 minutes

COOKING TIME
2–3 minutes

INGREDIENTS
300g green beans
pinch of salt

PASTE
2 Tbsp black sesame seed
  powder
4 tsp brown sugar
4 tsp soy sauce

Goma-ae is a Japanese side dish of vegetables in a sesame seed paste. Here I'm using black sesame seed powder for its unique nutty taste. This dish also works well with broccoli, cauliflower, asparagus or any seasonal vegetable.

METHOD
To make the paste, mix together black sesame seed powder, brown sugar and soy sauce. Set aside.

Bring a pan of water to the boil, add beans and a pinch of salt and cook for 2–3 minutes. Drain and cut off the ends. Set aside to cool.

Once beans have reached room temperature, add the sesame seed paste to the beans.

Serve in a bowl to share.

コールスロー

JAPANESE COLESLAW

SERVES
2–3

PREPARATION TIME
5 minutes

INGREDIENTS
2 handfuls of shredded
  green cabbage
2 handfuls of shredded red
  cabbage
4 Tbsp Japanese
  mayonnaise
flaky sea salt, to taste
white pepper, to taste

I love this recipe as it is so simple yet beautiful, so it is a perfect accompanying side dish. Try this with everybody's favourite dish, teriyaki chicken (page 170), or with honey soy spare ribs (page 172). You will see lots of happy faces around your dining table!

METHOD
Mix all the ingredients together in a bowl.

Serve on a large plate to share.

きんぴらごぼう
STIR-FRIED BURDOCK
'KINPIRA-GOBOU'

SERVES
2–3

PREPARATION TIME
5–10 minutes

COOKING TIME
10 minutes

INGREDIENTS
250g burdock
1 Tbsp sesame seed oil
2 Tbsp soy sauce
2 Tbsp brown sugar
chilli powder

Kinpira-gobou is a well-known side dish in Japan. As a people we love not only the taste but also the texture of burdock. This root vegetable has been used as a remedy for centuries throughout Asia – it also has the benefit of being low in calories and is a great sauce of fibre. If you can't find the burdock, you can substitute carrot, or lotus.

METHOD

Scrub the skin off the burdock lightly with a sponge or the back of your knife.

Slice burdock and then julienne finely. Soak in water for a couple of minutes.

Heat oil in a frying pan over medium–high heat.

Drain burdock and add to pan. Stir-fry for 2 minutes or until softened.

Add soy sauce and sugar and stir-fry for 5 minutes or until no liquid is left in pan.

Sprinkle with chilli powder and serve in a bowl to share.

茶碗蒸し
JAPANESE
STEAMED EGG BOWLS
[CHAWANMUSHI]

You might expect this to be sweet, but it is a savoury dish. In Japanese 'chawan' means bowl and 'mushi' means to steam. So chawanmushi is a steamed egg custard in a small bowl or ramekin that we serve as a side dish. We traditionally enjoy subtlety of taste and are particularly enamoured with the silky texture of steamed egg. To create this smooth texture, make sure to leave a little gap between the lids and bowls when steaming (so the lids are not completely closed).

METHOD

Arrange chicken, prawns and carrot in 4 ramekins.

Dissolve dashi in 40ml hot water and then mix with 350ml cold water.

Crack eggs in large bowl and beat well. Add dashi water, mirin and soy sauce. Season with salt and mix well.

Gently pour custard through a colander into ramekins.

Place 2 cups (500ml) water in a large pot or pan with a lid. Place ramekins in the water and bring the water to the boil. Reduce heat to low–medium. Place the lid on the pot. Insert a long chopstick between one side of the lid and pot so some steam can escape and create a smooth surface on the custards. Steam for 12–15 minutes or until egg custard is cooked.

Serve with teaspoons.

SERVES
4

PREPARATION TIME
10 minutes

COOKING TIME
15 minutes

INGREDIENTS

30g chicken, cut into small pieces

8 raw prawns, peeled and deveined

¼ carrot, sliced

1 tsp dashi powder

3 eggs

1½ tsp mirin

1 tsp soy sauce

salt, to taste

ゴマだれサラダ

SEASONAL SALAD
WITH SESAME SEED DRESSING

SERVES
4

PREPARATION TIME
25 minutes

COOKING TIME
nil

INGREDIENTS

SALAD
½ sunny (fancy) lettuce
¼ purple cabbage, shredded
¼ head of broccoli,
   blanched and refreshed in
   cold water
¼ telegraph cucumber
handful of watercress
segments of 1 orange
small handful of walnuts

DRESSING
2 Tbsp roasted sesame
   seeds
3 Tbsp Japanese
   mayonnaise
1 Tbsp rice vinegar
2 tsp soy sauce
1 tsp mirin
1 tsp peanut butter
1 tsp sugar
pinch of dashi powder

I use a traditional Japanese mortar and pestle to grind the sesame seeds for this dressing (but a regular one works just as well). The dressing is nutty and sweet, with an interesting citrus tang, and goes very well with any seasonal salad or simple steamed vegetables.

METHOD

Arrange salad ingredients on a large plate.

To make dressing, grind sesame seeds with a mortar and pestle or spice grinder. Transfer to bowl and mix with rest of dressing ingredients. Serve with salad.

ポテトサラダ

POTATO SALAD

SERVES

2

PREPARATION AND COOKING TIME

15 minutes

INGREDIENTS

800g potatoes, peeled and
  cut into large blocks
¼ onion, finely sliced
iced water
⅛ telegraph cucumber,
  halved and finely sliced
1 tsp table salt
2 Tbsp tinned corn kernels
4 Tbsp Japanese
  mayonnaise
1 Tbsp Japanese or
  American mustard
sea salt and white pepper,
  to taste

This simply made salad is great as a side dish or even in the lunch box. You can try using pumpkin instead of potato.

METHOD

Cook potatoes in a large pan of boiling water, drain, mash and set aside to cool down.

Soak onion in iced water for 2 minutes. Drain.

Sprinkle cucumber with salt and massage in, then set aside for 2 minutes. Squeeze excess water from cucumber.

Mix together mashed potato, onion, cucumber, corn, mayonnaise and mustard. Season with sea salt and white pepper. Keep in fridge until you serve.

茄子のおひたし

EGGPLANT, ROASTED AND MARINATED

SERVES
2

PREPARATION TIME
5 minutes plus 30 minutes marinating

COOKING TIME
30 minutes

INGREDIENTS
2 eggplants

SAUCE
1 tsp dashi powder
1 Tbsp brown sugar
2 Tbsp soy sauce
2 Tbsp cooking sake
1 red chilli, chopped

I often make this in large portions and keep in the fridge as it lasts for a couple of days. Our family always makes sure to have small side dishes ready in case unexpected (and hungry!) guests arrive.

METHOD
Preheat oven to 180°C.

Place eggplant on a baking tray and roast for 30 minutes or until cooked through. Alternatively, if you have a gas cooktop, you could cook the eggplant on an open flame for 8–10 minutes until cooked through. This will give the eggplant a beautiful smoky flavour.

Meanwhile, put dashi powder, sugar, soy sauce and sake in a small saucepan with 180ml water and bring to boil to dissolve dashi and sugar. Turn off the heat, add the chilli and set aside.

Peel skin off eggplant and discard. Halve the eggplant and put the halves in container with a lid, pour sauce over the top and leave in fridge to marinate for at least 30 minutes.

Slice to serve.

揚げ出し豆腐

AGEDASHI TOFU

This is a traditional Japanese tofu dish. 'Age' means 'deep-fried' and 'dashi' refers to the savoury broth. The key to this dish is to serve it as soon as you've deep-fried the tofu, otherwise it can turn soggy very quickly.

METHOD

Put tofu on a plate and cover with paper towel. Put another plate on top to compress tofu and leave for 15–20 minutes to remove moisture.

To make broth, put dashi powder, soy sauce, mirin and 1 cup (250ml) water in a small saucepan and bring to the boil. When dashi has dissolved, remove from heat, add grated ginger, cover pan to keep warm and set aside.

Cut tofu into quarters or smaller pieces if you prefer.

Heat oil in a large pan or deep-fryer. Coat tofu with starch and deep-fry for 2 minutes or until golden-brown and crispy. Drain on paper towel.

To serve, place tofu in small bowls and pour in broth. Garnish with bonito flakes and spring onion.

SERVES
4

PREPARATION TIME
10 minutes

COOKING TIME
5 minutes

INGREDIENTS
345g block firm tofu
canola or rice bran oil, for deep-frying
corn or potato starch
bonito flakes, to garnish
1 spring onion, finely chopped, to garnish

BROTH
½ tsp dashi powder
1 Tbsp soy sauce
2 tsp mirin
¼ tsp grated ginger

卵焼き
EGG ROLL
WITH SPRING ONION

SERVES

2

PREPARATION AND COOKING TIME

10 minutes

INGREDIENTS

4 eggs

1 tsp soy sauce

2 tsp mirin

2 spring onion, chopped

pinch of dashi powder or
  salt

1 Tbsp oil (any type except
  olive oil)

This is lovely, but a little fiddly in the pan: if you want to make it the easy (but much less impressive!) way, cook scrambled egg-style instead of making a roll. Also, when in season, I use asparagus here instead of spring onion.

METHOD

Crack eggs into a bowl and lightly beat. Add soy sauce, mirin, spring onion and dashi or salt, and mix well.

Place a small frying pan (traditionally we use a square frying pan for this in Japan) over medium heat and add oil (alternatively, use a non-stick frying pan).

Pour one-third of egg mixture into frying pan and spread around. Use chopsticks to stir gently as egg cooks.

When egg is about 80 per cent cooked, slide chopsticks or a spatula under it and fold in 1–2cm from one end. Keep folding in the same way until egg is in a roll (as in the picture).

Push egg roll to the far end of the pan and add another third of the egg mixture to pan (please make sure new egg mixture touches the rolled egg). As before, wait until the egg is 80 per cent cooked and then start rolling the egg roll over the new flat mixture to make an even larger single roll.

Push egg roll to far end of pan, add rest of egg mixture and cook as above until you have one large egg roll.

Slide egg roll onto a chopping board and slice to serve.

茄子と味噌のグリル焼き

EGGPLANT, CHARGRILLED WITH MISO AND CHEESE

SERVES
4

PREPARATION TIME
5 minutes

COOKING TIME
10 minutes

INGREDIENTS

2 eggplants, cut into 2cm
thick slices

2–3 Tbsp oil (any type
except olive oil)

25g mozzarella cheese

2 Tbsp panko (Japanese
breadcrumbs)

aonori (seaweed flakes) or
chopped parsley, to taste

MISO SAUCE

4 Tbsp white or mixed miso

4 Tbsp Japanese
mayonnaise

4 tsp mirin

I find the combination of miso and eggplant irresistible,
and topping with cheese gives an extra rich flavour. For a
different mix, try zucchini or steamed mussels instead of
the eggplant.

METHOD

Preheat grill or oven to high. Meanwhile, to make miso sauce, combine
miso, Japanese mayonnaise and mirin.

Heat a chargrill pan or frying pan over high heat. Brush eggplant slices
with oil on both sides and place on pan for 1–2 minutes. Turn over, cook
for another 1–2 minutes and then transfer to a baking tray.

Spread 1 tablespoon miso sauce over each eggplant slice and sprinkle
with cheese, panko and aonori or parsley.

Grill or bake for 2–3 minutes until cheese melts. Serve immediately.

サーモンの南蛮漬け

SUGAR AND SPICE
SALMON

SERVES
4

PREPARATION TIME
15 minutes

COOKING TIME
5 minutes

This salmon is called 'nan-ban-zuke' in Japanese and every single family has their own recipe. This is my family's secret version and I'm happy to share it with you. It's a great dish for a hot summer day – sweet and sour, but with a spicy kick from the chilli. Enjoy with a glass of your favourite white wine.

INGREDIENTS
500g salmon with skin, bones removed
½ cup plain flour
canola or rice bran oil, for deep-frying

SAUCE
300ml rice vinegar
180ml soy sauce
4 Tbsp cooking sake
4 Tbsp brown sugar
1 red chilli (fresh or dried), chopped
½ onion, finely sliced
½ red capsicum, finely sliced
½ green capsicum, finely sliced
½ yellow capsicum, finely sliced

METHOD
To make sauce, mix together the vinegar, soy sauce, sake, sugar, chilli, onion and capsicums, and set aside.

Cut salmon into cubes and dust with flour, shaking off excess.

Heat oil to 180°C in a deep frying pan and deep-fry salmon for 1–2 minutes. (Alternatively, you can pan-fry for a couple of minutes.)

Drain salmon of excess oil and place in bowl of sauce. Mix gently.

Serve in a large bowl to share, or in soup spoons as party finger food.

ロール白菜
CHINESE CABBAGE ROLLS

In Japan we call Chinese cabbage 'hakusai' and use it in a large number of different dishes. If you can't find hakusai, just use regular cabbage. You can also use minced pork or fish instead of chicken.

METHOD

Blanch Chinese cabbage in boiling water for 10–20 seconds or until softened.

Mix together mince, mushrooms, spring onions and soy sauce in a bowl and season with salt and white pepper. Divide into 8 small portions and roll into egg shapes.

Place a cabbage leaf on a flat surface (stalk end closest to you) and place a meatball at stalk end. Fold in both sides of leaf and roll up from stalk end to top. Seal with a toothpick.

Place all cabbage rolls in a large saucepan and add soy sauce, mirin, dashi and 1 cup (250ml) water. Bring to the boil, reduce heat, cover pan and simmer for 5-8 minutes.

MAKES
8 small rolls

PREPARATION AND COOKING TIME
15 minutes

INGREDIENTS
8 Chinese cabbage leaves
200g chicken mince
2 dried shiitake mushrooms, soaked in hot water for 10 minutes and chopped
2 spring onions, chopped
1 tsp soy sauce

SAUCE
1 Tbsp soy sauce
1 Tbsp mirin
1 tsp dashi powder

ハマグリの酒蒸し

SAKE AND LEEK-STEAMED DIAMOND CLAMS

SERVES
2–3

PREPARATION TIME
10 minutes plus 30 minutes
soaking

COOKING TIME
10 minutes

INGREDIENTS
800g diamond clams
salt or lemon slices
100ml cooking sake
½ leek, finely chopped
juice of 1 lime

Sake? Kampai! But sake, like wine, is not only for drinking, but is also an essential ingredient in many dishes. Cooking sake helps tenderise meat and seafood, and also brings out the 'umami' of the ingredients. Umami is the fifth element of taste – the others being sweet, sour, bitter and salty. The best English translation I can find for the wonderful and mysterious umami is 'pleasant savoury taste'.

METHOD

Soak clams in salted or lemon water for 30 minutes, making sure clams are completely covered. Rinse under cold water and drain.

Put clams and sake in a saucepan, put lid on and bring to the boil.

Reduce heat to medium and simmer for 3–5 minutes until clams have opened. Discard any that don't open. Add leek and cook for another 1–2 minutes before turning off heat.

Place clams with sake and leek in serving bowl and squeeze lime juice on top.

豚のチャーシュー
PORK CHA-SHU

SERVES
4-6

PREPARATION TIME
10 minutes plus overnight marinating

COOKING TIME
1 hour

INGREDIENTS

1kg boneless pork ribs

30g ginger, sliced

2 spring onions, green part only

180ml soy sauce

90ml mirin

90ml cooking sake

1 Tbsp sugar

2 Tbsp honey

Cha-shu is pork cooked and marinated in a sweet soy sauce. The longer you can marinate the meat, the better the taste will be. You can slice this and add to your favourite noodle dish or chop into small cubes for stir-fried rice.

METHOD

Roll pork and tie with string.

Place pork, ginger and spring onions in a large pot and cover with water. Bring to boil and then simmer over low heat, uncovered, for 45 minutes–1 hour. Skim impurities from surface of stock. Measure 180ml of stock and set aside.

Place a saucepan over high heat and add soy sauce, mirin, sake, sugar, honey and the 180ml stock. Bring to the boil.

Add pork to saucepan and cook in the sauce over medium heat for 10 minutes. Remove from heat and leave until cooled down.

Slice to serve or put pork with sauce in a zip-lock plastic bag or container and refrigerate overnight. Remember, the longer you marinate the pork, the better the taste will be.

焼き鳥3種
YAKITORI SKEWERS

MAKES
8 skewers each

PREPARATION TIME
10 minutes

COOKING TIME
15 minutes

CHICKEN SKEWERS WITH SOY

200g chicken mince

2 garlic cloves, grated

2 dried shiitake mushrooms,
  soaked in hot water for
  10 minutes and chopped

1 spring onion, chopped

2 tsp soy sauce

1 Tbsp plain flour

SAUCE

2 Tbsp soy sauce

2 Tbsp brown sugar

chilli flakes, optional

SOY BUTTER CORN SKEWERS

2 corn cobs, boiled and each
  cut into 4 pieces

knob of butter

1 Tbsp soy sauce

**PORK AND SPRING ONION
SKEWERS**

200g pork belly, cut into
  2–3cm lengths

4 spring onions, white
  part only, cut into 2–3cm
  lengths

'Yakitori' means 'chargrilled chicken', but also refers to the style of cooking. The method means threading ingredients onto skewers and then barbecuing or chargrilling. For each recipe you will need 8 wooden skewers, soaked in water before use to prevent burning during cooking.

CHICKEN SKEWERS WITH SOY METHOD

Preheat chargrill pan or barbecue to high.

Mix together sauce ingredients and set aside.

Mix together chicken mince, garlic, mushrooms, spring onion, soy sauce, flour and salt and white pepper. Divide mixture into 8 portions and shape each one around a skewer.

Lay tin foil on top of chargrill or barbecue and leave mince skewers on top to cook for 5 minutes or until cooked through. Turn skewers occasionally and brush with sauce.

SOY BUTTER CORN SKEWERS METHOD

Preheat chargrill pan or barbecue to high.

Thread corn onto 8 skewers and chargrill or barbecue for a couple of minutes until lightly charred.

Spread butter over corn and brush with soy sauce.

Cook for another minute before serving.

PORK AND SPRING ONION SKEWERS METHOD

Preheat chargrill pan or barbecue to high.

Thread pork and spring onion onto 8 skewers (2 pieces of pork and 2 pieces of spring onion per skewer).

Chargrill or barbecue for couple of minutes or until cooked through, turning occasionally. Season with white pepper and sea salt flakes.

人参と豆の肉巻き
WAGYU BEEF PARCELS

My mum made this often when we were children, for dinner and even for lunch boxes. The best meat to use is wagyu beef with its intense marbling – it will absolutely melt in your mouth. If you can't get wagyu, then use schnitzels, but be sure to tenderise them well.

METHOD

If you are using wagyu, cut into 2mm thick slices. If you are using schnitzels, tenderise with back of your knife.

Place meat on a flat surface and put 3 green beans and 3 carrot sticks at end closest to you. Roll up beef from closest end to make rolls.

Heat oil in a medium-sized saucepan over medium heat. Place all beef rolls in pan to sear.

Add sugar, sake and soy sauce to pan with 300ml water and bring to boil. Reduce heat to medium and simmer for 5–10 minutes.

Remove rolls from pan. Bring leftover sauce to the boil.

Mix starch with 1 tablespoon water and add to sauce. Stir over heat for 30 seconds until sauce has thickened. Pour over beef rolls to serve.

MAKES
4

PREPARATION TIME
10 minutes

COOKING TIME
15 minutes

INGREDIENTS

300g wagyu beef or 4 beef schnitzels

12 green beans

1 carrot, cut into thirds, and then into batons

1 tsp oil (any type except olive oil)

3 tsp brown sugar

1 Tbsp cooking sake

1½ Tbsp soy sauce

1 tsp potato starch or cornflour

イカめし

SQUID STUFFED WITH RICE AND PEAS

MAKES
4

PREPARATION TIME
10 minutes

COOKING TIME
10 minutes

INGREDIENTS

2 Tbsp soy sauce

1 Tbsp mirin

1 Tbsp cooking sake

2 tsp brown sugar

½ tsp grated ginger

300g cooked short- or
  medium-grain rice

2 Tbsp frozen peas,
  defrosted

4 frozen squid tubes,
  defrosted

This is a famous dish from the west coast of Japan. The people of that area use uncooked rice to fill the squid and then cook it for 40 minutes in a soy-based sauce. My recipe is a simplified version that takes just 10 minutes to cook.

METHOD

Mix together soy sauce, mirin, cooking sake, sugar, ginger and 100ml water.

In a separate bowl, mix together rice, peas and 1 tablespoon of the soy/sake mixture.

Stuff rice mixture into squid tubes with a spoon and seal with toothpicks (see page 96).

Place stuffed squid tubes in a saucepan, pour in the soy/sake mixture and drape a cartouche of baking paper on top of the squid, as shown in the pictures (see pages 94–95). Place over high heat and bring to boil. Reduce heat to low and simmer for 5 minutes. Flip the squid over and cook for another 5 minutes.

To serve, slice squid and drizzle sauce on top.

1
2
3
4

5 6
7 8

雨降って地固まる

AME FUTTE JI KATAMARU

Meaning: After the rain, the earth hardens. (That is, adversity builds character. After a storm, things will stand on more solid ground than they did before.)

JAPANESE CUISINE + MY FOOD PHILOSOPHY

Japan and Tokyo are the crowning country and capital of the culinary world, surpassing France and Paris with their number of restaurants with three Michelin stars. However, as the dust settles from the usurping of the crown from the traditional king, it is important to remember that the finest food from the finest chefs always has a humble beginning. In my opinion, some of Japan's best-kept foodie secrets can be found in its traditional country inns and within the homes of loving families.

PRINCIPLES OF JAPANESE CUISINE

No other country on Earth places as much importance as Japan on the process of preparation and the presentation of food.

Being famous in the modern world as the home of technological innovation, the quest for perfection naturally has made its way onto people's plates. I don't think that it is just the ingredients, seasoning or techniques alone that set our cuisine apart, but also the combination of appearance and presentation of food.

We have a saying that you enjoy a meal with your sight first, and with taste second. The skilful arrangement of food on appropriate and beautiful tableware adds so much to the enjoyment of the meal that it sometimes cannot be stressed enough. You may find in many Japanese restaurants, foods are often served in small portions, artfully arranged on individual dishes. We love to give consideration to how the colours and textures of foods served together complement each other, and this adds to the richness and depth of the dining event. However, in my personal opinion, it's the company that rounds off the dining experience the most.

Blended with this is the dichotomy that while one should seek perfection in the presentation and appearance of a dish, this does not necessarily mean complicated is best – quite the opposite. I maintain a personal philosophy, in line with Zen teachings, that there is power in simplicity. Much like how silence can sometimes tell you more than verbose conversation.

From our stone gardens to a final plated dish, we love subtlety. I often find that people tend to pile everything onto a plate believing elaborate presentation is better, but sometimes one ingredient in the dish can bring out more flavour, aroma and texture, and highlight the other ingredients. A great example is the use of daikon (Chinese radish). I often cook this humble vegetable in a dashi stock (made from bonito/tuna) and water for 20 to 30 minutes. You can taste every bit of the juice of the stock within the daikon when you take your first bite.

The Japanese culture is also reflected in the diet. My family is from a farming and fishing community, and so the produce plays an integral role in the day-to-day life that shapes the beliefs and attitudes of the community. Each region of the country retains its own local food specialties, from the Hokkaido prefecture in the North right to Okinawa in the South.

MY FOOD PHILOSOPHY

My personal philosophy is that 'no one can keep a bad mood around good food'. I believe that if you have a bad day at work or the kids have had a trying day at school, if you come home to find that someone has made you a home-cooked meal, it can almost instantaneously lighten your outlook and mood! When my husband is hungry, he is grumpy and irritable, so my secret to soothing him is to get him fed well and give him company. I've never seen anyone angry after eating a great meal.

All of my personal feel-good memories always involve food. Barbecues with our friends, picnics with my family, giant rice balls for breakfast in the mountains bordering our family home, or simply nice hot coffees with my mum and aunty while watching the sun rise ... the list is endless.

Because of what I do, I don't get invited to dinner a lot; people seem to find cooking for me nerve-wracking. And when I do get invites, I have so little free time that I often have to decline. This is a serious problem that I am trying hard to rectify! In my opinion, tasty food is as important as great company. As diligent Japanese, both my parents used to work very late, but they always made it a point when they came back home to ensure that we would be at the table together as a family. This meant no television during mealtimes – just talking, laughing and occasionally (or regularly!)

Courtesy of Sachie Nomura

fighting over food. All good memories. Hence the final element of my philosophy is simply 'sharing is caring': food shouldn't be made for a single person – it should be made to share.

鯛も一人はうまからず
TAI MO HITORI HA UMAKARAZU

Even sea bream is not delicious when eaten in loneliness.

PRINCIPLE OF FIVE KEY INGREDIENTS

The five ingredients that are essential for Japanese cooking are: soy sauce, cooking sake (ryorishu), mirin, miso and dashi (Japanese stock). Every Japanese household will have these ingredients in its own pantry. If you want to expand your repertoire, my recommendation is to add rice vinegar, Japanese mayonnaise (affectionately know as yum-yum sauce) and wasabi. With these core ingredients you can pretty much create the vast majority of popular Japanese dishes.

THE SECRET TO LONG LIFE

People often comment to me that Japanese people don't seem to put on weight and are renowned for long life – especially people from Okinawa! One of the secrets is the diet the Japanese people have eaten at home for the past thousand years.

The three main dishes in a Japanese meal are rice, miso soup and pickles, with a high consumption of fish, vegetables, seaweed and soy bean products. Rice is one of the major food groups and almost certainly the most prevalent staple food, but we make sure our meals are very well-balanced with these accompaniments. Often a meal is also proportionately heavy with vegetables, fish and other seafood, which are non-fattening foods compared to meat. Often these are grilled, steamed or made into a soup, so have either no or low fat content. Rice also contains very little fat and it is rare for most

Japanese to regularly consume cereal or crackers. That's why Japanese people aren't fat even though they eat white rice!

Also, Japanese cooking does not traditionally use much oil – this is to allow the natural flavour of the ingredients to make their way to your tastebuds. While we do enjoy a multitude of different techniques to cook fish (such as grilled, pan-fried, in stew, in soup or dried), sashimi or raw fish is an iconic delicacy enjoyed by Japanese and Japanophiles.

My mum says that when people are young, they need lots of energy to run around and be boisterous – that is, be kids! – so they have a massive craving for meat and substantial meals. However, as people age, this craving changes. We tend to move from meat – beef, pork and chicken – to a diet heavy in fish and seafood. When a Japanese person hits 30 to 40 years of age, they tend to eat seafood-based meals two to three times a week.

My parents are now in their early 60s and live out in a rural area in the Toyama prefecture, bordering a mountain range. They tend to their own vegetable gardens in the back yard and their diet mainly comprises of fish and vegetables. They eat meat only once or twice a week, unless they are entertaining guests.

腹八分目
HARA HACHI BUN ME
Eat to 80 per cent full

Another secret tip: eat to 80 per cent full. I was told that it takes 20 minutes, after the last morsel is swallowed, for the brain to register that the stomach is full.

Often my parents would say 'chew well, eat slowly', and they would always engage us in conversation while we sat at the table eating. They'd ask about what we did at school, and then actively listen to our answers, so the dining table became a family social event. This also served to slow down the pace of eating, so at the end of the night we would never feel bloated and go to sleep on an excessively filled tummy.

DESSERT CULTURE

Green tea and fresh fruits may follow a Japanese meal, but (contrary to Western practice) desserts are traditionally not served after meals, except in fine restaurants. This is not to say we don't appreciate desserts (I do!), but eating to excess after the main dishes is a rare occurrence. There are sweets (wagashi/yogashi) unique to Japanese cooking, but these are intended to accompany tea, rather than to follow a meal. Dessert is often around 3pm – called 'oyatsu' time.

When I first arrived in New Zealand, I lived with a family who fed me dessert every night. I ate banana sundaes, multiple scoops of ice cream, sticky date puddings, and cornflakes and strawberry jam. (Japanese are not always able to say 'No' when to refuse generosity might offend.) Needless to say I put on weight: 12 kilograms within three months. I adopted this habit of eating dessert, with tea or coffee, after every meal because it tasted so good, and when I returned to Japan to visit my family I asked my mum for a cup of coffee and biscuits after dinner, which shocked my parents no end! My mum's response: 'Have you forgotten that you're Japanese? We don't eat dessert after dinner!' This was the first time I realised the cultural culinary differences between Japan and New Zealand.

THE FIFTH TASTE

Most people have heard of salty, sweet, sour and bitter – but umami? What is this unusual word? If you have a passion for food, like me, then chances are you've eaten a delicious steak (wagyu beef, for example) at some point. Here's a fun, and potentially frustrating, exercise: close your eyes and think of that first bite. The texture, the aroma, the sheer chewy pleasantness. Okay, good, but what about the taste? How on Earth do you describe it? We Japanese have a term for that. What you're tasting is 'umami' (pronounced 'oo-mommy'), a term coined by a famous food-lover and chemist, which translates as 'pleasant, savoury taste'.

Seafood, steak and mature cheeses all have the signature of umami, and even foods such as soy beans and corn contain it too.

For a bit of a science lesson: when meat (for example) begins to cook on an open flame, the proteins are broken apart while undergoing molecular change. One of these molecules is L-glutamate and it is this molecule that is responsible for umami. We were always taught that our tastebuds were equipped to detect sweet, sour, salty and bitter, but of course our tongue knew better.

The first documented occurrence of umami began some 1000 years ago, when my forefather Japanese cooks began adding certain types of seaweed to soup stocks, and although they didn't know why it happened, it greatly enhanced the flavour. Umami is richness and complexity, and in Mother Nature's kitchen it's the best flavour-enhancer too. Quite simply, it makes food much more delicious. Umami – the mysterious, and sometimes elusive, fifth taste.

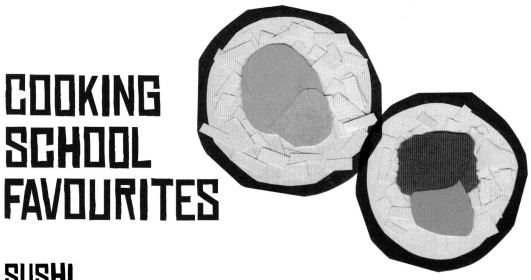

COOKING SCHOOL FAVOURITES

SUSHI

Sushi is now one of the most popular snack foods in the world and has iconic status globally. Interestingly, sushi actually originated in Southeast Asia rather than Japan. I read that over 2400 years ago, fish was preserved by fermenting it with a combination of rice and salt. Somewhere along the line Japanese started consuming the rice with raw fish and this has consequently found its way to becoming the national dish of Japan.

One thing I find fascinating is Westerners' obsession with sushi – one can go to almost any city in the world, stand in the CBD at lunchtime and watch office workers carrying full or half-eaten plastic boxes with sushi inside! Prior to arriving in New Zealand, I only ate sushi on special occasions such as Autumn festivals, birthdays and New Year's celebrations.

FOUR KEY TYPES OF SUSHI

1) MAKI SUSHI
The most common sushi that you see – where the sushi is rolled into a tube and cut into equally sized circles. (For recipe, see page 120.)

2) TEMAKI SUSHI
Temaki or hand-rolled sushi ('te' meaning 'hand'

and 'maki' meaning 'to roll') is most commonly done at home. It's easy for entertaining, as you simply create a cone with the seaweed and fill with your favourite fillings – it's fantastic for children or roll-your-own-sushi parties. (For recipe, see page 124.)

3) NIGIRI SUSHI
Nigiri can be described as small rice balls created by hand with seafood on top. The most common types of seafood used are tuna, eel, snapper, salmon or scampi.

4) INARI SUSHI
Inari sushi is a simple and inexpensive type of sushi, in which sushi rice is filled into cooked and marinated aburaage (deep-fried tofu) bags. It is actually named after the Shinto god Inari, who is believed to have a fondness for fried tofu. (For recipe, see page 40.)

SOME SUSHI FACTS THAT YOU MAY FIND INTERESTING

1. Ever wondered how much wasabi you should add to your sushi? Traditionally, the serving chef will make that decision for you but these days it's more up to your personal tastebuds. So when the restaurant serves it on the side

for you to use at your own discretion, just be careful not to overdo it or you will have what I call the 'wasabi experience' – not pleasant, but it will clear all your sinuses for sure!

2. It is important to know that not all sushi is created the same – traditional nigiri sushi is made so that the entire piece can be consumed in one bite, and etiquette considers this the correct way to eat it. Outside of Japan, it is unusual to eat nigiri sushi directly with your hands. Typically chopsticks are used for sashimi, nigiri sushi, and maki sushi. Hands are only used for temaki sushi.

MISO SOUP

I don't think there are many other things that can warm you up on a cold day or night better than a hot, steaming bowl of miso soup. This is a traditional Japanese soup consisting of a stock called 'dashi', into which softened miso paste is mixed. Miso is a paste made from a mixture of soy beans, a starch (such as rice or barley), salt, water and yeast. This mixture is traditionally placed into wooden barrels and aged for as long as six months to three years; this method of preparation can be traced back to Buddhist monks from the 7th century.

Depending on personal preference and regional and seasonal recipes, many different ingredients are added – my favourite is 'tara' (cod) miso soup, which is famous in Toyama, the prefecture where my parents live. We use all parts of the cod – the head, bones, liver, etc. – and while it is quite expensive, it makes for a soup that is perfect for winter.

Miso is rich in fibre, protein, vitamins and minerals, so it is not surprising that miso soup

was used regularly by Samurai warriors for its nutritional content. Indeed, miso is also very high in antioxidants that can help prevent aging, and the wakame seaweed added to miso soup can also help to lower blood pressure and reduce cholesterol. Consequently, it is a culinary staple in Japan. (For tofu and wakame miso soup recipe, see page 39.)

EGG ROLL

Tamagoyaki (literally 'pan-fried egg'; also called 'dashimaki') is a type of Japanese omelette. It is made with eggs, dashi, soy sauce and sugar or mirin, to give it a slightly sweet taste. This mixture is then gradually added to a pan, and the layers of cooked egg are rolled. These are usually cooked in a special rectangular pan.

You often find this in lunch boxes – my mum used to make this all the time. My favourite inclusions was spring onions. My fondest memories are of when we would have picnics with tamagoyaki – and to be extra naughty I would cover it with Japanese mayonnaise! (For egg roll with spring onion recipe, see page 76.)

KATSU

Katsu was invented in the late 19th century – it was actually introduced to Japan by the Portuguese. It consists of a breaded, deep-fried cutlet, traditionally pork or chicken, that is 1–2cm

thick and sliced into bite-sized pieces, generally served with shredded cabbage and/or miso soup.

I love to eat katsu with tonkatsu sauce, which is like a type of thick Japanese Worcestershire-style sauce. It is also popular as a sandwich filling or (my husband's favourite) served with Japanese curry and a big bowl of rice as katsu don – an informal, homely, one-bowl lunchtime dish. (For pork katsu with sweet miso sauce recipe, see page 162.)

TEMPURA

Tempura is the Japanese method of deep-frying, which was introduced to Japan by Portuguese missionaries in the 16th century. The Portuguese had a dish of deep-fried shrimp that they called 'tempero', which is likely where the name 'tempura' came from. An interesting fact is that pre-tempura, pan-frying any meal was very rare in Japanese cuisine, and it wasn't until the 19th century that it was considered socially acceptable by high society and, consequently, tempura restaurants became more prevalent throughout the country.

The ingredients and styles of cooking and serving tempura vary greatly from region to region, with importance being placed on using fresh, seasonal ingredients. Our family favourites are prawn, oyster mushroom, broccoli, eggplant and any herbs that we picked off the mountain. (For recipe, see page 150.)

DIPPING SAUCE
Tempura is served with a dipping sauce called 'ten-tsuyu', which is made of soy sauce, mirin and dashi – the customer adds daikon to their personal preference. The tempura should only be dipped lightly into this.

SOBA (BUCKWHEAT) NOODLES

'Soba' means 'buckwheat' in Japanese, so soba noodles are a type of thin noodle made from buckwheat flour, water, and a combining agent such as yam or konjac. Unlike udon noodles, the colour of soba noodles is usually grey.

For those who haven't travelled to Japan, the summer climate for most of the country is very hot and humid. To combat the heat, a number of dishes meant to be eaten cold have been developed. One of the main cold summer dishes is soba noodles, which is particularly popular when the weather becomes unbearable. In Japan, eating special soba noodles on New Year's Eve is a favourite custom. This delectable dish is called 'toshikoshi' (literally 'year-passing') soba and it symbolises, as the name indicates, the previous year's passing.

About 10 years ago, my friend's mother was visiting from Japan and I received an invitation from her for a special soba lunch. My answer was an immediate 'I am leaving home right now!' When I arrived at their place, it actually turned out to be more of a working session rather than an eating one. Within minutes, my friend's mother was pointing at me and telling me to cook the soba and each of my friends were allocated kitchen tasks, from washing the cooked soba noodle, to plating up, to serving the other guests in the living room. One of my friends was even given a stop-watch to monitor the cooking time!

The taste must have been good but I only remember the pressure the old lady put on me! (For duck noodles recipe, see page 144.)

ONIGIRI [RICE BALL]

Onigiri is a Japanese food made from rice, formed into triangular or oval shapes and often wrapped in nori (seaweed). This dish traces back centuries to when onigiri was used as a quick meal – because it was simple to make and very filling. Many Samurai were known to store simple rice balls, flavoured with salt and wrapped in bamboo leaves, as a timely lunchtime meal during war. Now, there are myriad different fillings, such as sweet soy kelp called 'kombu', salted salmon, katsuobushi (bonito flakes), or (my favourite) a simple pickled ume (umeboshi).

I have been noticing that onigiri have become very popular among builders and tradespeople in New Zealand and Australia, who traditionally would eat pies and chips that would be laden with fat. The great advantages are the simple fillings that normally wouldn't be deep-fried, the convenience and, even better, that they aren't messy!

OKONOMIYAKI

I love okonomiyaki, and I don't know anyone who doesn't. Okonomiyaki is a type of Japanese savoury pancake that is made with a wide range of ingredients. The name is derived from the words 'okonomi', which means 'what you like' or 'what you want', and 'yaki', which means 'grilled' or 'cooked'. Unlike Western pancakes they are not sweet and fluffy, but are usually filled with chopped cabbage, shrimp, pork, squid, yam and/ or kimchi. Perhaps a better description than savoury pancake is to call it a Japanese pizza.

If you visit Japan, I strongly recommend that you go to an okonomiyaki restaurant – it is an experience in itself. This is the only type of restaurant (that I know of) where the waiter and waitress will ask you if you want to cook for yourself (at the table or teppan) or if you want them to cook. What other restaurant will ask you this kind of question when you go and pay to have cooked meals? Originally, I didn't think this was strange, but when I was explaining this to our friends I suddenly realised what a great idea this is – customers are happy because they can cook themselves (without cleaning) and the staff don't get complaints afterwards! Perfect! (If you are cooking okonomiyaki at home, you don't need a teppan: you can use a normal frying pan, just like you would cook a pancake.)

Each region in Japan is fiercely proud of their variations of this dish – this is known as the 'pride of okonomiyaki'. There are two main variations of okonomiyaki: Osaka-style (also called Kansai-style) and Hiroshima-style.

For Osaka-style okonomiyaki, you mix ingredients such as cabbage, spring onion, pork, squid (basically whatever you like) with batter, which consists of mainly flour, egg, water and grated yama imo (Chinese yam). Yama imo is very sticky and slimy when grated, and this works as a combining agent.

For Hiroshima-style okonomiyaki, ingredients are not mixed with batter. Instead, they first make a thin crepe with the batter and then different ingredients are put on top. Some regions add noodles (yakisoba) as well. An interesting aside: in the late 1940s, when Japan was recovering from the aftermath of World War II, food was scarce, particularly in Hiroshima. The ever-resourceful citizens of Hiroshima would use metal sheets from the ruins to cook wafer-thin pancakes piled with as much chopped cabbage as possible. Thus began the first 'Hiroshima-yaki'.

Try both styles of okonomiyaki and see which you prefer, and have fun with the ingredients. You might even invent your own style! (For recipe, see page 154.)

TERIYAKI

Teriyaki chicken is the number one Japanese class in my cooking school. We hear story after story, either emailed to us or from students we bump into on the street, about how much students' families love our teriyaki recipe.

The word 'teriyaki' derives from the words 'teri', which refers to the sheen or lustre from the sugar and mirin, and 'yaki', which means 'grilled' or 'cooked'. Tip: teriyaki can also be served cold, as it is often a dish found in bento boxes and makes for a great lunch.

You can buy pre-made teriyaki sauce in a bottle, but an authentic sauce is actually very easy to make when you know how. One instance that always warms my heart is when a lady called me to rave about how well the recipes worked for her and her family and thank me for her time at Sachie's Kitchen. That Christmas she had an idea for a novel, personalised gift: home-made teriyaki sauce, bottled, wrapped and labelled with personalised names for all of her friends. I get goose bumps when I hear these kinds of stories – it tells me and my team that we are doing something right, and that we are contributing to Kiwis trying some interesting food. (For teriyaki chicken recipe, see page 170.)

AGEDASHI TOFU

Agedashi tofu is where silken (kinugoshi) firm tofu is cut into cubes, lightly dusted with starch (either potato or corn), deep-fried and served in a savoury broth.

Agedashi tofu is an old and revered dish. An interesting aside: it was included in a 1782 Japanese all-tofu cookbook entitled *Tofu Hyakuchin* (literally meaning: 'One hundred tofu'). Along with chilled tofu (hiyayakko) and simmered tofu (yudofu), agedashi tofu is among the simplest of common tofu dishes. (For recipe, see page 75.)

SUNOMONO

'Su' means 'vinegar', so 'sunomono' is the Japanese word for 'vinegared things' and refers to a variety of pickled dishes. It has a refreshing taste to cleanse the palate and so makes a great side dish. (For cucumber and celery pickles recipe, see page 32. For Namasu and Hakusai pickles recipes, see page 34.)

GYOZA [JAPANESE DUMPLING]

Gyoza is a popular dumpling in Japan, and is one of my family's favourite dishes.

One thing that my (Chinese) husband perpetually makes a song and dance about is the fact that the Chinese get credit for the invention of this little dumpling, which was said to have been introduced to Japan in the late 17th century. However, since then, gyoza has become so popular that there

are gyoza restaurants and even a Gyoza Stadium located in Osaka, Japan! The Gyoza Stadium has a museum complete with history and explanations of the many varieties of this adopted dish.

Gyoza can be cooked in various ways: deep-fried, boiled, steamed or pan-fried. Boiled gyoza and steamed gyoza are soft and eaten hot. Deep-fried gyoza can be finger food, so it's great for entertaining, but the most common way to cook gyoza is by pan-frying. The most popular gyoza fillings include pork, cabbage and garlic chives, but feel free to experiment. I have heard of gyoza being dessert dumplings and having fillings of chocolate and bananas before! (For recipe, see page 166.)

TATAKI

Many people associate tataki with the manner of preparing fish or meat, as it literally means 'pounded' or 'hit into pieces'. However, when this word is used to describe the dish, it means the meat (usually beef) or fish (usually tuna) is seared very briefly over an open flame or in a hot pan, sliced thinly and served with different sauces. My favourite one is a soy sauce base.

My husband is not a big beef-eater, but when it comes to beef tataki, that habit is discarded very quickly. He loves to eat the seared beef simply with a side dish of salmon sashimi and a hot bowl of Japanese rice. If he eats that, I know he will be satisfied until at least the next day and I have a happy husband! (For tuna tataki recipe, see page 51. For beef tataki salad recipe, see page 54.)

WAGYU BEEF TATAKI

If you want to be a little more extravagant, use wagyu beef when making your tataki. Wagyu ('wa' meaning 'Japan' and 'gyu' meaning 'beef') is the most expensive and, in my opinion, the most succulent beef in the world. Known worldwide as the 'caviar of beef', it is characterised by its intense marbling, naturally enhanced flavour, tenderness, juiciness and, hence, price!

Unlike many restaurants in the West, in Japan some of the best food comes from establishments that are secret and hidden. When my husband and I were visiting Kobe a couple of years ago, we walked around town without a plan, searching for something to eat. It was almost 7pm and our tummies were grumbling. I happened to look up and saw a tiny little sign saying 'Steak House' in a small window of the fifth floor of a totally nondescript building. Kobe city is famous for Kobe beef and I knew that we had to try it, so we took a lift to the fifth floor, knocked and asked for a menu (we just wanted to make sure that we could afford it first). The proprietor said there was no menu here, but he could serve us a Kobe beef dinner set-menu for ¥6900 (just under NZ$90) per person. Without hesitation we entered the tiny 10-seater restaurant while being quizzed by the proprietor about how we knew about the place, because customers only went there by referral.

He was the chef, waiter and company for the entire meal, as he served salad as an entrée and

seared the Kobe beef in front of us on a teppan (served with little seasoning) with garlic fried rice. Simple, but to die for! To this day my husband recounts the experience with excitement, full of the satisfaction of finding a secret hideaway and also of sampling such succulent Kobe beef.

Some of the legends around authentic wagyu beef:

- The cattle is fed beer. The yeast from the beer helps their digestion and increases their appetite. I guess this increases the fattiness!

- The cattle is massaged to relieve stress and muscle stiffness. It is believed that the eating quality of the meat is directly correlated to how calm and relaxed the cattle is.

- Some people also play music to relax the cattle.

All of this makes eating wagyu a must-tick experience for any foodie.

ステーキハウス

舞彩
MAYA

笑いは人の薬

WARAI-WA HITO-NO KUSURI

*Meaning: A good laugh is
people's medicine.*

MAINS

This is a collection of my favourite main dishes – when I grew up in Japan, I inherited these recipes from my family and later gave them my own twist. Now they are yours to enjoy with your friends and family.

I want to say try them ALL, but my personal favourites are okonomiyaki, ramen noodles with soy broth, gyoza and seafood hotpot! What will your favourites be?

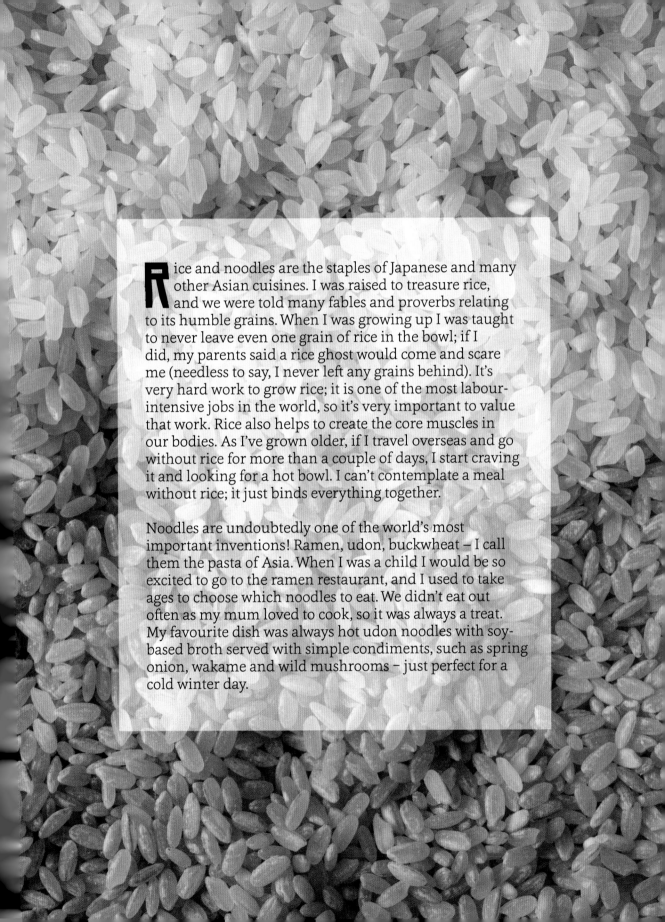

Rice and noodles are the staples of Japanese and many other Asian cuisines. I was raised to treasure rice, and we were told many fables and proverbs relating to its humble grains. When I was growing up I was taught to never leave even one grain of rice in the bowl; if I did, my parents said a rice ghost would come and scare me (needless to say, I never left any grains behind). It's very hard work to grow rice; it is one of the most labour-intensive jobs in the world, so it's very important to value that work. Rice also helps to create the core muscles in our bodies. As I've grown older, if I travel overseas and go without rice for more than a couple of days, I start craving it and looking for a hot bowl. I can't contemplate a meal without rice; it just binds everything together.

Noodles are undoubtedly one of the world's most important inventions! Ramen, udon, buckwheat – I call them the pasta of Asia. When I was a child I would be so excited to go to the ramen restaurant, and I used to take ages to choose which noodles to eat. We didn't eat out often as my mum loved to cook, so it was always a treat. My favourite dish was always hot udon noodles with soy-based broth served with simple condiments, such as spring onion, wakame and wild mushrooms – just perfect for a cold winter day.

HOW TO COOK RICE

SERVES
4–5

MAKES
5½ cups of cooked rice

PREPARATION TIME
5 minutes

COOKING TIME
20 minutes

INGREDIENTS
2 cups short- or medium-
  grain rice

Rice is the staple of every Asian household. Cooking it is a simple process, but very important – it not only binds the meal together but also forms part of our heritage. My mother wouldn't let me do anything in the kitchen until I had mastered how to cook rice properly.

METHOD
First, wash the rice. Put it in a pot, fill with cold water, swirl the rice around and then drain away the milky water.

Now, use the palm of your hand to push the rice around a couple of times (we believe your soul goes into the food). Add water, swirl the rice again and drain the milky water. Repeat a couple more times until the water is clear.

Drain the rice completely and place in a rice cooker or pot. Add 2 cups (500ml) clean water (1 cup rice to 1 cup water) and soak for 30 minutes before cooking.

Turn on the rice cooker. If cooking in a pot, cover with a lid, place over high heat and bring to the boil. As soon as it boils, reduce heat and simmer for 15 minutes. Turn off the heat and leave for 5 minutes before removing lid of the pot. Perfect rice!

すし酢

SUSHI ZU
[SUSHI VINEGAR]

MAKES
75ml (5 Tbsp)

PREPARATION TIME
5 minutes

COOKING TIME
nil

INGREDIENTS
3 Tbsp rice vinegar
2 Tbsp sugar
1 tsp salt

This sushi vinegar is used to season the rice for making sushi. One cup of raw rice makes 450–480g cooked rice (i.e. 2½ cups of cooked rice, enough to make two sushi rolls). The ratio I use is roughly 1 part sushi vinegar to 10 parts cooked rice, so for 450g cooked rice, I add 45ml (or 3 tablespoons) of this sushi vinegar.

METHOD
Mix together all ingredients until sugar and salt dissolve.

巻き寿司
MAKI SUSHI

MAKES
16 pieces (2 rolls)

PREPARATION TIME
10 minutes

COOKING TIME
10 minutes

INGREDIENTS
400g freshly cooked short-
or medium-grain rice
2½ Tbsp sushi vinegar (use
ready-made or see recipe
on page 118)
2 nori sheets
soy sauce, to serve
wasabi, to serve

SALMON AND AVOCADO ROLL
150g raw, sashimi-grade
salmon, cut into strips
¼ avocado, sliced

SALAD ROLL
150g surimi, chopped
and mixed with 2 Tbsp
Japanese mayonnaise
⅛ cucumber, cut into sticks
⅛ capsicum, cut into sticks
50g purple cabbage,
shredded
few fancy lettuce leaves

Making a sushi roll is just like riding a bicycle. Once you've learnt how to do it, the skill is yours forever. So, if the first one doesn't come out right, don't worry – practice will make perfect!

METHOD

Put warm rice in a large non-stainless steel bowl. Add sushi vinegar and mix well with a cutting action to prevent rice becoming mushy. Try to coat each rice grain. Cover with a wet cloth.

Place a nori sheet on sushi rolling mat. Wet your hands so rice does not stick, and put half the sushi rice on the nori.

Spread rice evenly, leaving a 1cm border at end furthest from you.

Place salmon and avocado on the rice at end closest to you.

Lift up closest end of mat, upwards and over the filling, using your fingers to keep the ingredients in the centre of the roll. As the rice meets the nori, squeeze the roll to make it firm and lift the top edge of the mat out to stop it getting caught in the roll. Keep rolling until complete and squeeze the roll again, as shown in the pictures (see pages 122–123). Rest the roll for a couple of minutes to ensure the nori sticks together.

Wet knife with water and cut each roll into 8 pieces. Serve with soy sauce and wasabi.

Repeat with remaining rice, nori and filling to make salad roll.

5 6
7 8

手巻き寿司
TEMAKI SUSHI

SERVES
4

PREPARATION TIME
30 minutes

COOKING TIME
nil

INGREDIENTS

900g (5 cups) cooked short- or medium-grain rice

6 Tbsp sushi vinegar (use ready-made or see recipe on page 118)

20 nori sheets, split in half

1 avocado, sliced

50g carrots, cut into julienne

100g cucumber, seeded, cut into strips

½ red capsicum, cut into strips

185g tin tuna, drained, mixed with 1–2 Tbsp Japanese mayonnaise

200g sashimi-grade salmon slices

50g surimi, chopped, mixed with 1 Tbsp Japanese mayonnaise

100g butter or fancy lettuce

soy sauce, to serve

wasabi, to serve

sushi ginger, to serve

'Te' means 'hand' and 'maki' means 'to roll', hence 'temaki sushi' means 'hand-rolled sushi'. This style of sushi is great if you are hosting a party and cooking for lots of people. It's also fresh, different and especially appealing to kids. Once you've prepared the ingredients, show everyone how to hand-roll their sushi and then let them make their own. I've listed the ingredients I prefer, but feel free to include your own favourites (even beef steak).

METHOD

Put warm rice in a large non-stainless steel bowl. Add sushi vinegar and mix well with a cutting action to prevent rice becoming mushy. Try to coat each rice grain. Cover with a wet cloth.

Arrange filling ingredients on plates.

Place a nori sheet on your hand, scoop 1–2 tablespoons of rice and put on the right-hand side of the nori. Spread with your spoon over right half of the nori.

Place your preferred filling ingredients on top of the rice.

Roll up from the right side into a cone shape, as shown in the pictures (see page 126). Dip into soy sauce and enjoy with wasabi and ginger.

1 2
3 4

初心忘れるべからず
SHOSHIN WASURERU BEKARAZU

Meaning: We should not forget our beginner's spirit. (That is, we shouldn't forget the excitement or humility in starting something new.)

チラシ寿司
CHIRASHI SUSHI

SERVES
4-6

PREPARATION TIME
15 minutes

COOKING TIME
15 minutes

INGREDIENTS

½ carrot, diced

6 dried shiitake mushrooms, soaked in 400ml warm water (save soaking water) and sliced

1 tsp dashi powder

2 tsp mirin

2 tsp cooking sake

2 Tbsp soy sauce

1 tsp sugar

1 tsp oil (any type except olive oil)

1 egg, beaten

5½ cups cooked genji mai (brown rice) or short- or medium-grain rice

100ml (6½ Tbsp) sushi vinegar (use ready-made or see recipe on page 118)

50g green beans, blanched and sliced on the diagonal, to garnish

salmon roe, to garnish (optional)

Using a mat and nori (seaweed) sheets is not the only way to prepare sushi. This chirashi sushi is one of my favourite ways to celebrate special occasions such as weddings, anniversaries, birthdays and festivals. It's a colourful and exciting dish to share with your family and friends.

METHOD

Put carrot, shiitakes, dashi, mirin, sake, soy sauce, sugar and the 300ml shiitake water in a pot. Bring to the boil and then simmer for 5–10 minutes. Set aside to cool.

Place a small frying pan over medium heat and add oil. Pour about half the egg into the pan to make a thin omelette. Remove when cooked and make another one or two. Cut into julienne strips and set aside.

Put warm rice in a large non-stainless steel bowl. Add sushi vinegar and mix well with a cutting action to prevent rice becoming mushy. Try to coat each rice grain. Cover with a wet cloth.

Squeeze liquid from carrots and shiitake and mix with the rice. Place rice on a large plate and spread julienned omelette on top. Garnish with green beans and salmon roe.

椎茸と卵の雑炊

JAPANESE RISOTTO
WITH MUSHROOM AND EGG

We often have this Japanese risotto when we're not feeling well – like the proverbial chicken soup. Or when we've over-indulged and have cravings for a simple, clean, vegetarian meal. You can serve this with pickles.

METHOD
Rinse cooked rice in a colander under cold water to remove starch and drain.

Put dashi, soy sauce and sea salt in a pan or clay pot with 2 cups (500ml) water. Bring to the boil, add mushrooms and rice and stir just once (if you stir many times the water will become cloudy). Bring back to the boil.

Pour eggs into pan on top of the rice. Add spring onion and turn off heat. Put lid on pan immediately to steam egg and spring onion. Leave for 2 minutes.

Serve with flaky sea salt and shichimi.

SERVES
2

PREPARATION TIME
5 minutes

COOKING TIME
10 minutes

INGREDIENTS
260g (1½ cups) cooked
   short-grain rice
1 tsp dashi powder
2 tsp soy sauce
½ tsp sea salt
50g wild mushrooms or
   shiitake mushrooms
2 eggs, beaten
1 spring onion, sliced on the
   diagonal
flaky sea salt, to serve
 shichimi powder (Japanese
   seven chillies), to serve

3色弁当
THREE-COLOUR LUNCH BOX WITH SALMON

SERVES
1

PREPARATION TIME
5 minutes

COOKING TIME
15 minutes

INGREDIENTS

1 bowl of cooked rice
oil, for cooking (any type except olive oil)
100g salmon, cut into small pieces
1 tsp plain flour
4 tsp sugar
2 Tbsp soy sauce
1 egg, lightly beaten
pinch of salt
⅓ green capsicum, cut into julienne

When I was at school, my mum made lunch boxes every morning for me and my younger brother, and this was one of our favourites. Sometimes I couldn't wait until lunchtime and ate mine during morning break. Make your family the envy of their classmates or co-workers!

METHOD

Place rice in lunch box or container.

Heat a small pan over medium–high heat and add 1 tablespoon oil. Dust salmon with flour, and pan-fry for 1–2 minutes each side until cooked. Add 2 teaspoons sugar and 1 tablespoon soy sauce to pan and cook for another couple of minutes to caramelise. Set aside to cool down.

Heat 1 tablespoon oil in a frying pan over medium–high heat. Season egg with a pinch of salt and add to pan. As soon as egg starts to cook, use a wooden spoon to move it around and break up into small lumps. Set aside to cool down.

Put capsicum and remaining 2 teaspoons sugar and 1 tablespoon soy sauce in a small pan over high heat and bring to the boil. Reduce heat to low and simmer for a couple of minutes. Set aside to cool down.

When all food has cooled down, place salmon, scrambled egg and capsicum on top of rice in lunch box. Don't forget to take your chopsticks or a fork to eat with.

Tip: You could substitute the salmon with chicken mince.

親子丼

OYAKO-DON [CHICKEN AND EGG STEW ON RICE]

SERVES
1

PREPARATION TIME
5 minutes

COOKING TIME
8 minutes

INGREDIENTS

½ tsp dashi powder

1 tsp soy sauce

½ tsp mirin

½ tsp cooking sake

¼ onion, sliced

½ chicken thigh, cut into small pieces

1 egg, lightly beaten

1 spring onion, chopped

1 bowl of cooked rice

shredded nori, to garnish

In Japanese 'oya' means 'parent' and 'ko' means 'child', hence the name for this chicken and egg dish! It is a very simple yet tasty meal and great for a quick lunch or dinner.

METHOD

Put dashi, soy sauce, mirin and cooking sake in a small saucepan with 100ml water, and bring to the boil. Reduce heat to medium, add onion and chicken, and cook for couple of minutes or until chicken is cooked through.

Increase heat to high. Pour egg and spring onion into the pan, cover with a lid and cook for 30 seconds. Slide the chicken egg on top of the rice.

Garnish with shredded nori.

手作りうどん
HOME-MADE UDON NOODLES

SERVES
3-4

PREPARATION TIME
35 minutes plus 1–2 hours
resting dough

COOKING TIME
5–7 minutes

INGREDIENTS
2½ cups plain flour
1 Tbsp salt
1 spring onion, chopped,
  to garnish
shichimi powder (Japanese
  seven chillies), to garnish
toasted sesame seeds, to
  garnish
shredded nori, to garnish

BROTH
3 Tbsp soy sauce
2 Tbsp mirin
1 tsp dashi powder
pinch of salt

This is a great recipe to make with your children, as it's hands-on (and feet-on!) and, as we all know, kids love to eat what they've made themselves. Home-made udon noodles simply taste better and have a lovely chewy texture. This dish is the recipe I make for my husband whenever he is craving something simple and cooked with love. This dough makes around 450g noodles – enough for 3 to 4 people.

METHOD
Mix together flour, salt and 180ml water. Once the dough starts to hold together, put it in a zip-lock bag. Now it is ready for kneading!

Place a tea towel on the ground and put bag of dough on top and cover it with another tea towel. Take off your shoes and step on the bag with your feet. Once the dough is flattened, open the plastic bag and fold the dough a couple of times, and then knead again with your feet. Repeat this for 20 minutes (see page 138).

Remove dough from bag, put in a bowl and cover with a wet cloth. Leave for 1–2 hours. If it's a cold day, warm the oven to 40°C and leave the bowl inside for an hour.

To make broth, in a medium-sized pot over high heat, add 5 cups (1.25 litres) of water, soy sauce, mirin, dashi powder and salt to taste. Bring to the boil, then turn heat down and leave broth to simmer until you're ready to serve.

Let's make udon noodles! Dust bench with flour and place dough on bench. Use your palm to flatten dough and then use a rolling pin to flatten to 2mm thickness.

Fold dough and cut into 2mm wide strips. (See also pages 138–139 for step-by-step photos.)

Boil 2 litres water in a large pan and cook noodles for 5–7 minutes or al dente. Drain and rinse under cold water.

Put noodles in serving bowls, pour in hot broth, and garnish with spring onion, shichimi, sesame seeds and nori.

1 2
3 4

醤油ラーメン
RAMEN NOODLES WITH
SOY BROTH

If you are a noodle lover, you must try this soy-based noodle soup. It may look time-consuming, but once you've made the broth it only takes 15 minutes to whip things up! The great and rewarding thing about this recipe is you make around 3 litres of stock, which can be frozen when it's cooled down, as you only need half of it for the noodles. You will also be surprised to see spaghetti transformed into ramen noodles ...

METHOD

To make stock, rinse chicken and pork bones under cold water. Place in a large pot with water to cover. Bring to the boil and cook for couple of minutes – all the impurities will be floating on top.

Drain the water and rinse the bones again. Wash the pot and put bones back in. Add the ginger, onion, garlic, carrot, spring onion and enough hot water to cover. Bring to the boil and turn heat to low and simmer for 1 hour uncovered. Strain through a colander.

Put all noodle soup ingredients in a pot with 1.25 litres stock (freeze the rest), bring to the boil and simmer until ready to serve.

Cook noodles as instructed on packet. If you are using spaghetti, boil 2.8 litres water in a large pot and add baking soda. Cook spaghetti for 10–13 minutes or until al dente, then drain. (You will see colour and smell of spaghetti change to that of ramen noodles.)

Meanwhile, heat a frying pan and add 1 teaspoon of sesame oil. Stir-fry bean sprouts quickly and season with pepper and salt. Place noodles and soup in serving bowls and serve with bean sprouts, eggs (cut into halves), wakame and spring onion.

SERVES
3–4

PREPARATION TIME
10–15 minutes

COOKING TIME
15 minutes plus 1 hour for cooking broth

INGREDIENTS
4 bundles ramen noodles or 240g spaghetti plus 2 Tbsp baking soda
100g mung bean sprouts
2 hard-boiled eggs
wakame, softened
2 spring onions, white part only, chopped

STOCK
4 chicken carcasses
1 pork bone
1 knob of ginger, sliced
1½ onions, cut into quarters
3 garlic cloves, halved
1 carrot, cut into quarters
2 bunches spring onions, green part only

NOODLE SOUP
50ml soy sauce
40ml cooking sake
1 tsp sugar
1 tsp salt
½ tsp white pepper
1 tsp dashi powder

味噌ラーメン
HOT MISO RAMEN SOUP

SERVES
4

PREPARATION TIME
5 minutes

COOKING TIME
15 minutes

INGREDIENTS

150g chicken mince
1 Tbsp tobandjan (chilli bean sauce)
1 Tbsp gochujang (Korean chilli paste), optional
15g butter
3 garlic cloves, finely chopped
1 Tbsp finely chopped ginger
2½ Tbsp white (or mixed) miso
2 tsp brown sugar
2 Tbsp soy sauce
2 Tbsp mirin
½ tsp dashi powder
4 portions wavy egg noodles (or 4 packets instant noodles)
2 hard-boiled eggs, cut in half, to garnish
wakame, soaked in water for 1 minute and drained, to garnish
2 spring onions, chopped, to garnish
sweet corn kernels, to garnish

I have to admit to being a noodle addict, and ramen are my favourites. There are many different stocks to make the soup base, such as miso, soy, salt (a clear broth) and tonkotsu ('pork bone' – a cloudy white broth). Most Japanese noodle shops spend hours and hours making and perfecting these stocks, but I can't wait that long! Try my hot miso ramen in 20 minutes.

METHOD

Mix chicken mince with tobandjan and gochujang (if using) in a small bowl and set aside to marinate.

Place a wok or large pan over high heat and add butter. When melted, add garlic and ginger and stir-fry until aromatic.

Add chicken mince and stir-fry for 2–3 minutes until chicken is cooked.

Add 1.2 litres water, bring to the boil and add miso, sugar, soy sauce, mirin and dashi powder. Stir until dissolved and then simmer over low heat.

Meanwhile, boil another 1.2 litres water in a large pan and cook noodles as instructed until al dente. Drain and place in serving bowls.

Add miso soup to bowls and garnish with egg, wakame, spring onion and corn kernels.

鴨せいろ
DUCK NOODLES
[KAMOSEIRO SOBA]

SERVES
4

PREPARATION TIME
10 minutes

COOKING TIME
20 minutes

INGREDIENTS
4 bundles buckwheat/soba
   noodles
2 duck breasts, skin scored
2 spring onions, sliced
   diagonally

DIPPING SAUCE
150ml soy sauce
150ml mirin
1 Tbsp brown sugar
½ tsp dashi powder
shredded nori, to garnish
shichimi (Japanese seven
   chillies), to taste

Who doesn't love noodles? There are so many varieties to choose from! For this dish, I use buckwheat noodles (called 'soba' in Japan) with succulent duck breast. Soba noodles are made of buckwheat, wheat, salt and water, and whenever I eat them, no matter what my mood, I feel centred by their deliciously earthy taste.

METHOD
Preheat oven to 180°C.

Cook noodles in boiling water as per instructions on package. Drain and refresh under cold water to stop cooking.

To make dipping sauce, mix soy sauce, mirin, sugar and dashi powder with 2 cups (500ml) water in a small saucepan and bring to the boil. Reduce heat and simmer for 3 minutes. Remove from heat.

Cook duck breasts (skin side down first) for 5 minutes in a frying pan over medium heat. (You don't need any oil in the pan as the duck skin will have enough.) Turn and cook other side for 2 more minutes.

Transfer duck breasts, skin side up, to an oven tray and cook in the oven for 5 minutes. Leave to rest for 2–3 minutes before slicing.

Add spring onions to the frying pan with the remaining duck oil and cook for 1 minute over medium heat. Add spring onion and duck oil to dipping sauce.

Arrange noodles on a serving plate with sliced duck, garnish with nori and shichimi, and pour dipping sauce into a small cup. To enjoy the dish, dip a duck slice and small amount of soba noodles into the sauce.

海鮮鍋
SEAFOOD HOTPOT

SERVES
4

PREPARATION
30 minutes plus 1–2 hours
resting sauce plus 15
minutes soaking konbu

COOKING TIME
15–20 minutes

INGREDIENTS
3 snapper fillets, cut into
   large cubes
8 scallops
8 diamond clams
¼ hakusai (Chinese
   cabbage), cut into bite-
   sized pieces
2–3 spring onions, sliced on
   the diagonal
1 carrot, sliced on the diagonal
250g mung bean sprouts
handful of mushrooms
   (oyster, wild, or shiitake)
350g firm tofu, cut into cubes
steamed rice, to serve

PONZU SAUCE
120ml soy sauce
80ml rice vinegar
40ml lime juice
2 Tbsp mirin
20g bonito flakes
5g konbu

STOCK
10g konbu
1 Tbsp dashi powder
1 Tbsp soy sauce

We enjoy eating hotpots in Japan over the winter season and the recipes for them are almost endless. For those of you who love to entertain, think about holding a 'mystery hotpot party' … guests bring whatever ingredients take their fancy and cook in a clay pot ('nabe').

METHOD
To make dipping sauce, mix soy sauce, vinegar, lime juice, mirin, bonito flakes and konbu in a jar and leave in the fridge for 1–2 hours. Strain through a colander. This can also be done the night before serving.

To make stock, pour 1.2 litres water into a large nabe (clay pot) or a saucepan and soak konbu for 10–15 minutes.

Place nabe or pan over high heat and bring to the boil, discarding konbu just before it starts to boil. Add dashi, soy sauce and pinch of salt to make the stock.

Add seafood to stock and cook for 2–3 minutes. Add vegetables and tofu, place lid on nabe or pan and cook for 10–15 minutes over medium–high heat.

Serve with steamed rice and ponzu sauce for dipping.

味噌鍋
MISO HOTPOT

This is a must-do dish for the middle of winter. It's a personal favourite of mine, because it's so great for sharing with your friends and family. I have listed my favourite ingredients here, but don't be afraid to add your own. If any is left over, I always add udon noodles and serve it again as noodle soup – the flavours blend together in the soup to make something altogether heavenly, and we are not going to waste this!

METHOD

To make stock, place a clay pot or large pan over medium–high heat and add butter.

When butter has melted, add garlic and ginger. Stir-fry until aroma is released.

Add 1.2 litres water, bring to boil and add miso, brown sugar, soy sauce, mirin and gochujang. Stir well to dissolve and soup stock is ready!

Add rest of hotpot ingredients to stock. Put lid on, bring to boil and then reduce heat to medium and cook for 10–15 minutes or until meat is cooked.

Place hotpot in middle of dining table and serve with steamed rice.

SERVES

4

PREPARATION TIME

10 minutes

COOKING TIME

20 minutes

INGREDIENTS

$\frac{1}{6}$ cabbage, cut into large pieces

$\frac{1}{6}$ Chinese cabbage, cut into large pieces

5 dried shiitake mushrooms, soaked in hot water for 5 minutes

350g firm tofu, cut into large cubes

2 handfuls of mung bean sprouts

500g sliced pork or chicken thigh

2–3 spring onions, sliced on the diagonal

200g kimchi (Korean picked cabbage), optional

steamed rice, to serve

SOUP STOCK

30g butter

3 garlic cloves, grated

1 Tbsp grated ginger

4 Tbsp miso

2 tsp brown sugar

2 Tbsp soy sauce

2 Tbsp mirin

1 Tbsp gochujang (Korean hot chilli paste)

天ぷら
TEMPURA

SERVES
4

PREPARATION TIME
10 minutes

COOKING TIME
10 minutes

One of the secrets to making good tempura is to use ice-cold water. Another trick I picked up from my mother is to add a little Japanese mayonnaise to the batter – this makes the consistency delightfully crisp. For best results, organise everything first and then deep-fry the tempura at the very end, serving and eating as soon as you can.

INGREDIENTS

canola or rice bran oil, for
  deep-frying
8 banana prawns, peeled
  and deveined
½ nori sheet, cut into
  4 pieces
1 capsicum, cut into 8 pieces
1 celery stalk, cut into
  4 pieces
½ red onion, cut into
  2 pieces
plain flour, for dusting
100g daikon, peeled and
  grated

DIPPING SAUCE

75ml soy sauce
75ml mirin
½ Tbsp sugar
¼ tsp dashi powder

TEMPURA BATTER

1 egg, lightly beaten
1 Tbsp Japanese
  mayonnaise
handful of ice cubes
1 cup plain flour

METHOD

To make dipping sauce, mix soy sauce, mirin, sugar and dashi powder with 1 cup (250ml) water in a small saucepan and boil for 1 minute. Reduce heat and simmer for a further 1–2 minutes. Remove from the heat and set aside.

To make tempura batter, beat egg and mayonnaise in a bowl with a pinch of salt and then add 250ml of water and ice cubes. Add half the flour and mix well. Add remaining flour and mix only a couple of times.

Heat oil in a wok or deep saucepan to 180°C.

Dust prawns, nori and vegetables with flour and dip lightly into batter. Deep-fry until crispy.

Drain on paper towel and serve hot with dipping sauce mixed with grated daikon.

鯛のグリル焼き

MISO-GRILLED FISH

SERVES
2

PREPARATION TIME
10 minutes plus 4 hours
marinating

COOKING TIME
10 minutes

INGREDIENTS
2 snapper fillets, with skin
4 Tbsp mirin
2 Tbsp cooking sake
4 Tbsp white or mixed miso
2 tsp sugar
steamed rice and miso soup,
  to serve

Instead of snapper here, you could use tarakihi, kahawai, trevally, mackerel or any other white fish. If you don't have a good grill for cooking the fish, heat a frying pan over medium heat, put tin foil in the frying pan (to avoid the fish being burnt) and place the fish on top. Cover with a lid and cook for 2 minutes, then flip the fish and cook the other side for a couple of minutes.

METHOD
Put mirin and sake in a small pan and bring to boil. Boil for 10 seconds, then remove from heat. Add miso and sugar and mix well. Set aside to cool.

Score fish on the skin side a couple of times, cover with paper towel and place in a zip-lock bag. Pour miso mixture into the bag, making sure it covers the paper towel, and seal bag.

Marinate fish in fridge for at least 4 hours.

Take fish out of bag and remove paper (do not wash fish).

Heat grill to high and place tin foil on a baking tray. Place fish, skin side up, on tin foil and grill for 10 minutes or until cooked through.

お好み焼き

OKONOMIYAKI
[JAPANESE PANCAKES]

SERVES
4

PREPARATION TIME
10 minutes

COOKING TIME
30 minutes

INGREDIENTS
½ small cabbage, finely
   chopped
4 spring onions, finely
   chopped
4 eggs
4 rashers bacon, chopped
16 raw prawns, peeled and
   deveined
oil, for frying (any type
   except olive oil)

BATTER
2 cups plain flour
2 tsp dashi powder
½ tsp soy sauce

TO SERVE (ANY OR ALL)
okonomiyaki sauce
Japanese mayonnaise
bonito flakes
aonori (seaweed flakes) or
   shredded nori

Okonomiyaki are much-loved Japanese savoury pancakes that can contain a variety of ingredients, which means you can pan-fry whatever you like. Okonomiyaki restaurants in Japan allow you to cook this yourself at the table. The dish originated in the Osaka region, but now people from all over the country have adapted okonomiyaki. You can buy okonomiyaki sauce to serve with this or make your own: mix 1 tablespoon Japanese mayonnaise with 1 tablespoon tomato ketchup and 1½ tablespoons Worcestershire sauce.

METHOD

To make batter, whisk flour, dashi and soy sauce with 2 cups (500ml) water in a bowl until smooth.

In another bowl, mix together quarter of cabbage, quarter of spring onion, 1 egg, 1 bacon rasher, 4 prawns and 1 scoop of batter. (This will make one pancake.)

Place a frying pan over medium–high heat and add a little oil. Spread mixture into a circle 1–1.5 cm thick in frying pan.

Cook for about 5 minutes or until bubbles start to form in middle of pancake and it is slightly browned underneath. Turn pancake with a spatula and cook for 3 minutes.

Cook rest of batter and filling to make another three okonomiyaki.

Serve with okonomiyaki sauce, mayonnaise and a sprinkling of bonito flakes and/or aonori.

ブロッコリーとエビチリ

GARLIC PRAWNS
WITH SPICY TOBAN SAUCE

This hot and spicy garlic prawn dish is irresistible. The best results, in my opinion, come from deep-frying the prawns first so they retain a moist and meaty texture. If you prefer not to deep-fry the prawns, stir-fry them with the ginger and garlic for a couple of minutes before adding the broccoli and toban sauce. And you can try other seasonal vegetables instead of broccoli.

METHOD

Coat prawns with starch.

Half-fill a deep frying pan with oil and place over medium–high heat. Deep-fry prawns for 1 minute and drain on paper towel.

Place a saucepan over medium–high heat and add 1 tablespoon oil. Add ginger, garlic and spring onion and stir-fry for 1 minute. Add deep-fried prawns and broccoli and stir-fry for 1 minute.

Mix together toban sauce ingredients and add to pan. Stir-fry for 1 minute to caramelise and then serve with steamed rice.

SERVES
2

PREPARATION TIME
10 minutes

COOKING TIME
5 minutes

INGREDIENTS

12 large raw prawns, peeled and deveined
2–3 Tbsp potato starch or corn starch
canola or rice bran oil, for deep-frying
1 Tbsp chopped ginger
2–3 garlic cloves, chopped
1–2 spring onions, white part only, chopped
small head of broccoli, cut into florets and blanched
steamed rice, to serve

SPICY TOBAN SAUCE

1 Tbsp tobandjan (chilli bean sauce)
1 tsp soy sauce
3 Tbsp tomato ketchup
2 tsp sugar
1 Tbsp cooking sake

海老フライ
DEEP-FRIED PANKO PRAWNS
WITH TARTARE SAUCE

SERVES
4

PREPARATION TIME
15 minutes

COOKING TIME
15 minutes

INGREDIENTS

12 raw prawns (I personally like to use banana prawns as they are a good size, but any type will do)

salt and pepper, to taste

5–6 okras

5–6 baby carrots

4 mushrooms, halved

1 cup plain flour

2 eggs, lightly beaten

2–3 cups panko (Japanese breadcrumbs)

1 Tbsp toasted sesame seeds

canola oil, for deep-frying

TARTARE SAUCE

¼ cucumber, seeded and finely chopped

¼ onion, finely chopped

1 hard-boiled egg (size 7), finely chopped

4 Tbsp Japanese mayonnaise

1 tsp rice vinegar

½ tsp soy sauce

white pepper and salt, to taste

Deep-fried prawns have always been a favourite of mine and this tartare sauce works superbly as a dipping sauce. Any seasonal vegetables are suitable for this dish, but my personal preferences are broccoli, capsicum and fresh shiitake or other mushrooms.

METHOD

To make sauce, put cucumber and onion in a colander, sprinkle over a teaspoon of salt and massage the salt into the mixture for a minute. Squeeze out the moisture from the mixture and transfer to a bowl. Add the egg, mayonnaise, vinegar and soy sauce, season with salt and pepper and mix well. Cover with plastic wrap and refrigerate until needed.

Peel and devein prawns. Rinse under cold water and pat dry with paper towel. Score the insides of prawns, flip over and flatten out with fingers to prevent prawns curling up during cooking. Season with salt and pepper.

Coat prawns and vegetables with flour, shaking off excess, dip into beaten egg and roll in breadcrumbs mixed with sesame seeds.

Heat oil to 180°C in a deep frying pan or wok.

Deep-fry prawns and vegetables in batches for 3–5 minutes or until golden brown. Drain on paper towel and serve hot with tartare sauce.

海老シュウマイ

PRAWN AND PORK
SHUMAI

MAKES
20

PREPARATION TIME
25 minutes

COOKING TIME
10 minutes

INGREDIENTS

1 Tbsp sesame oil
¼ onion, chopped
230g raw prawns, peeled,
  deveined and chopped
180g pork mince
4–5 garlic cloves, chopped
2–3 shiitake mushrooms,
  soaked in hot water and
  chopped
2 Tbsp oyster sauce
½ Tbsp soy sauce
ground white pepper, to
  taste
20 won ton wrappers
frozen peas, for garnish
chopped carrots, for garnish

Shumai originated in China and has made its tasty way through Japan and Southeast Asia. I hope you will enjoy this recipe as much as my family does. I have a tip for cooking these: place a baking sheet in your steamer before adding the shumai, to prevent them sticking.

METHOD

Heat oil in a frying pan or wok over medium heat. Add onion and sauté for 2 minutes until translucent and softened. Remove from heat and cool.

Put onion, prawns, mince, garlic, mushrooms, oyster sauce, soy sauce and white pepper in a large bowl and mix well with your hands.

Place 1 tablespoon of mixture in centre of a won ton wrapper. Gather wrapper around filling and hold gently with your hand so wrapper will stick to filling. Leave top unsealed.

Put frozen peas and/or chopped carrots on top of shumai and place in a steamer. Steam for 8–10 minutes or until cooked through.

味噌かつ

PORK KATSU
WITH SWEET MISO SAUCE

SERVES
4

PREPARATION TIME
15 minutes

COOKING TIME
15 minutes

INGREDIENTS

4 pork fillets (sirloin/scotch fillet)

salt and pepper, to taste

4 Tbsp plain flour

2 eggs, lightly beaten

1–2 cups panko (Japanese breadcrumbs)

canola or rice bran oil, for deep-frying

¼ cabbage, shredded, to serve

snow pea sprouts, for garnish

SWEET MISO SAUCE

50g red miso

50g sugar

2 Tbsp cooking sake

1 Tbsp mirin

My mum used to make this for good luck before exams or sporting events, as the word 'katsu' also means victory. People often use soy or Worcestershire sauce, but I love this sweet miso sauce.

METHOD

Tenderise pork with back of a knife. Season with salt and pepper.

Put flour, egg and panko in separate bowls. Dust pork with flour, dip into egg and coat with panko.

Half-fill a deep frying pan with oil and place over medium–high heat. Deep-fry the pork for 2–3 minutes on each side until golden. If the pork sizzles when you lift it out of the oil, then it's cooked. Drain on paper towel and cut into strips.

To make sauce, mix together miso, sugar, sake and mirin in a small pan over medium heat. Stir until sugar is dissolved and sauce is smooth. Set aside.

Drizzle sauce over pork and serve with shredded cabbage garnished with snow pea sprouts.

鶏肉のトマトソース炒め

CHICKEN WITH SAUTÉED SPINACH

Whenever my mum made this dish, my brother and I would always have a fight over who got the most. I wasn't a big fan of spinach when I was a child, but whenever my mum cooked this for us I ate a lot. It also makes a great lunch box the next day if there are ever leftovers.

METHOD

Put chicken in a small bowl with sake and garlic. Season with salt and white pepper, mix well, cover with plastic wrap and marinate in fridge for 30 minutes.

Place a wok over medium–high heat and add 1 tablespoon oil. Add spinach and cook for 2 minutes. Arrange spinach on a serving plate.

Add more oil to wok and drain chicken, keeping the marinade. Stir-fry chicken for 3–5 minutes or until brown. Add marinade, cover wok with lid and steam for a couple of minutes or until chicken is cooked through.

Add tomato sauce and Worcestershire sauce to wok and stir-fry until caramelised.

Place chicken with spinach and serve with steamed rice.

SERVES
2

PREPARATION TIME
10–15 minutes, plus
30 minutes marinating

COOKING TIME
15 minutes

INGREDIENTS

350g chicken thighs, cut into bite-sized pieces
3 Tbsp cooking sake
3 garlic cloves, grated
salt and white pepper, to taste
oil, for stir-frying (any type except olive oil)
200g English spinach
2 Tbsp tomato sauce
2 Tbsp Worcestershire sauce
Steamed rice, to serve

餃子

GYOZA
[JAPANESE DUMPLINGS]

MAKES
50 dumplings

PREPARATION TIME
40 minutes

COOKING TIME
15 minutes

INGREDIENTS
1 packet 50 gyoza wrappers

FILLING
⅛ cabbage
1 tsp salt
400 g lean pork or chicken
  mince
½ bunch garlic chives, finely
  chopped
4 dried shiitake mushrooms,
  soaked in hot water and
  finely chopped
1 Tbsp grated ginger
2 tsp soy sauce
2 tsp sesame oil, plus 2 tsp
  extra, for cooking
pinch of salt

DIPPING SAUCE
2 Tbsp soy sauce
2 Tbsp rice vinegar
la-yu (Japanese chilli oil),
  optional

I still have fond memories of learning to make these with my mum in our kitchen. Gyoza are very versatile – you can pan-fry, steam, boil or deep-fry them, or simply add a couple to your noodle soup. These dumplings also freeze well in zip-lock bags.

METHOD

Dice cabbage finely and sprinkle with 1 teaspoon salt. Give it a bit of a massage. Leave for 10–15 minutes and then squeeze with your hands to remove any moisture.

With your hands thoroughly mix together cabbage, mince, chives, mushrooms, ginger, soy sauce, sesame oil and pinch of salt.

Dry your hands completely (or wrappers will stick). Place a gyoza wrapper on one hand and put 1 teaspoon filling in centre of wrapper.

Brush edge of half the wrapper with cold water. Make a semi-circle by folding the wrapper in half. Pinch open sides of wrapper together with your fingers and seal the top, as shown in pictures (see page 168).

Place a large frying pan over medium–high heat, add 2 teaspoons sesame oil and arrange 20–25 gyoza in pan. Add 200ml water to cover bottom of pan, cover with lid and cook on medium–high heat for 6–7 minutes or until translucent, cooked and no liquid is left in pan. Take off lid and cook for another 30–60 seconds for the bottoms to go crunchy. Cook remaining gyoza or freeze them.

Mix together soy sauce, vinegar and chilli oil, if using. Serve gyoza hot with dipping sauce.

失敗は成功の元

SHIPPAIHA
SEIKOUNOMOTO

Meaning: Failure teaches success

照り焼きチキン

TERIYAKI CHICKEN

SERVES
4

PREPARATION TIME
5 minutes

COOKING TIME
20 minutes

INGREDIENTS
4 boneless chicken thighs
3 Tbsp plain flour
oil, for pan frying (any type
   except olive oil)
toasted sesame seeds,
   to garnish
steamed rice, to serve
Japanese coleslaw (see
   recipe on page 62), to
   serve

TERIYAKI SAUCE
35g brown sugar
75ml mirin
75ml cooking sake
75ml soy sauce

I have found through my cooking school feedback that teriyaki chicken is one of the most popular Japanese dishes. Don't feel you have to be restricted to chicken: the sauce goes well with beef, pork, salmon, or even stir-fried vegetables and tofu. If you like to think ahead, you could make extra sauce and keep it in your fridge.

METHOD
To make teriyaki sauce, mix sugar, mirin, sake and soy sauce in a small pan and bring to boil. Reduce heat to medium and simmer for 2 minutes. Set aside.

Score the chicken, flatten and dust with flour.

Heat oil in a pan over medium–high heat and cook chicken for 2–3 minutes, skin side down. Turn and cook other side for another 2–3 minutes or until cooked through.

Add teriyaki sauce to pan and cook until thickened and lightly caramelised.

Slice chicken, garnish with sesame seeds and serve with steamed rice and Japanese coleslaw.

金のためにここへ来るわけではないのだ。
「それでは私がここに来た理由を申し上げますわ」
正面に立っち、じっと背広の矢田貫其を見ていった。経営は凄く順調だ。単に

スペアリブ

HONEY SOY SPARE RIBS

SERVES
3–4

PREPARATION TIME
20 minutes

COOKING TIME
25 minutes

INGREDIENTS

1kg pork spare ribs
8 garlic cloves, grated
2 tsp black pepper
1 tsp sea salt
100ml soy sauce
100ml honey
1 Tbsp oil (any type except olive oil)

You can marinate pork ribs with all sorts of different spices and sauces, but sometimes it's nice to keep it very simple – soy sauce and honey are my choice of ingredients for this dish. These ribs are great to throw on the barbecue.

METHOD

Cover spare ribs with garlic, black pepper and salt and leave in fridge for 15–20 minutes.

Preheat oven to 180°C. Line a baking tray with baking paper.

Mix soy sauce and honey together.

Heat oil in a large frying pan over high heat. Cook spare ribs for 2–3 minutes on each side until browned.

Place spare ribs on baking tray and bake in oven for 10 minutes.

Brush ribs with honey soy sauce mixture and bake for another 5 minutes. Repeat 2 or 3 times if you like.

Put remaining honey soy sauce in a small saucepan and boil until caramelised.

Chop ribs into smaller lengths. Drizzle with caramelised honey soy sauce before serving.

豚の味噌漬け
MISO ZUKE
PORK SCHNITZEL

'Miso zuke' means to marinate meat, seafood or vegetables in a miso-based paste. This not only gives the meat a delectable flavour, but tenderises it at the same time. I serve this with lettuce leaves and steamed rice.

METHOD

Mix together miso, sake, mirin, sesame oil, garlic and yoghurt in a container.

Tenderise pork with the back of a knife. Add to container, stir to combine and leave in fridge to marinate for 2 hours.

Place a large frying pan over high heat and add oil. Fry pork schnitzel for a couple of minutes on each side or until cooked through (take care not to wash miso coating off the meat).

Serve with lettuce leaves and steamed rice.

SERVES
2

PREPARATION TIME
5 minutes plus 2 hours marinating

COOKING TIME
10 minutes

INGREDIENTS
400g pork schnitzel
1½ Tbsp white or mixed miso
1 Tbsp cooking sake
1 Tbsp mirin
1 tsp sesame oil
2 garlic cloves, grated
1 Tbsp plain yoghurt
2 Tbsp oil, for frying (any type except olive oil)
butter lettuce, to serve
steamed rice, to serve

蓮根のはさみ揚げ

DEEP-FRIED LOTUS ROOT
WITH BEEF

SERVES
3–4

PREPARATION TIME
20 minutes

COOKING TIME
20 minutes

INGREDIENTS
20–24 large pieces (about
 350g) frozen lotus roots
 (renkon)
1 Tbsp vinegar
300g beef mince
2 spring onions, chopped
1 egg
2 Tbsp plain flour
salt and black pepper, to
 taste
potato starch or corn starch,
 for dusting
canola or rice bran oil, for
 deep-frying

DIPPING SAUCE
soy sauce
Japanese karashi or
 American mustard

The unique texture of the lotus root is the highlight of this dish. Be sure to try it with the dipping sauce made of soy sauce and Japanese mustard. You can use pork or chicken mince instead of beef.

METHOD
Defrost lotus root and slice into 5mm thickness. Add vinegar to 1 litre cold water and soak lotus root in vinegar water to avoid discoloration.

Combine beef mince, spring onion, egg and flour and season with salt and black pepper.

Drain lotus root and pat dry with paper towel. Lay out on flat surface. Sprinkle with flour.

Place 1½ tablespoons mince mix on top of a lotus root slice and put another slice on top of the mince (flour side down) to make a sandwich. Press firmly so sandwich sticks together.

Dust sandwich with starch and deep-fry for 2–3 minutes until cooked through.

To make dipping sauce, mix together soy sauce and a bit of mustard. Serve with hot lotus root sandwiches.

味噌バターのアイフィレステーキ
MISO-BUTTER EYE FILLET
WITH EDAMAME PURÉE

SERVES
4

PREPARATION TIME
15 minutes

COOKING TIME
10 minutes

INGREDIENTS
4 beef eye fillets (approx. 180g each)
salt and pepper, to taste
oil, for frying (any type except olive oil)

MISO BUTTER
1 Tbsp white or mixed miso
50g butter, softened
zest of 1 lime

EDAMAME PURÉE
1 cup edamame beans
1 tsp dashi powder
½ tsp soy sauce
½ tsp wasabi powder, or to taste
pinch of salt

DASHI CARROTS
8 baby carrots, peeled
1 tsp dashi
1 tsp soy sauce

Let me introduce you to a different way to use edamame beans. These beans have a unique flavour and work very well with any meat of your choice. Miso butter is another weapon to add to your culinary arsenal – it has a distinctive taste that you'll absolutely want to have in your fridge at all times. Use it for simple vegetable stir-fries or try pairing it with scallops and leek.

METHOD
Preheat oven to 180°C.

For miso butter, mix together miso, butter and lime zest, cover with plastic wrap and place in freezer for 5 minutes or in fridge for 10 minutes to firm.

For edamame purée, mix beans, dashi, soy sauce and ½ cup (125ml) warm water and a pinch of salt in a food processor. Add wasabi powder to taste, and mix well.

Put carrots in a small pan over medium–high heat with dashi, soy sauce, 1 cup (250ml) water and a pinch of salt. Cook for 2–3 minutes or until carrots soften.

Season beef and pan-fry in a little oil for 1–2 minutes on both sides. Transfer to an oven tray, put two slices of miso butter on top of each fillet and cook for 3–5 minutes. Leave to rest for 5 minutes.

Serve 1 tablespoon edamame purée as a base on each plate, with miso-butter beef and dashi carrots.

GROWING UP IN JAPAN

THE INFLUENCE OF MY MUM AND AUNTY

It is not only my food influence, but who I am as a person today that can be tracked directly to my parents, particularly my mum. She is still my first and number one role model and, ever since I was a child, we have shared the same values and fit like peas in a pod.

蛙の子は蛙
KAERU NO KO WA KAERU

Literally: The child of a frog is a frog.

My mum and I spent a lot of time together in the kitchen when I was a child. My parents, unlike many Asian parents, actually never forced me to study, but they were still very strict on values, manners and making us to do sports! Being Japanese, we are used to hierarchy, and through sport we learnt about discipline, respecting others and how to work effectively in a team – all the important elements to live harmoniously in a Japanese society.

見目より心
MIME-YORI KOKORO

Goodness of heart is more important than appearance.

My grandma also possessed a very stern character – I know this as my parents used to talk about her often when I was a child. Both my grandparents on my dad's side passed away just before I was born, but my mum always told me that one thing that her mother instructed her was not to feed my father takeaway and to avoid ready-made foods.

Consequently, my mum took this to heart, and so eating out became a treat for me and my brother. We only went out for dinner maybe three or four times a year, as far as I can remember. The rest of the time, my mum was cooking at home or I was helping her with prep in the kitchen and making sure my younger brother didn't starve while my parents worked! To be honest, at first it felt like a chore, but now I miss those moments. I remember that I would perpetually use homework as an excuse for not being able to help my mum, while conversely telling my teacher that the reason that I didn't finish my homework was because I was spending all my time being 'mum' at home, cooking, getting laundry, and feeding my little brother!

My aunty is a massive foodie too and alongside my mum she must lay claim to being the biggest influence on my culinary skills today. She is always cooking for a large number of people, simply because everybody loves her food! Every time I return to Japan, I get to nourish my soul by spending time with both my mum and aunty and, of course, we are all in the kitchen, chatting and cooking. It's great to still be able to spend time with her in the kitchen, as even now I'm still corrected or even told off if anything is out

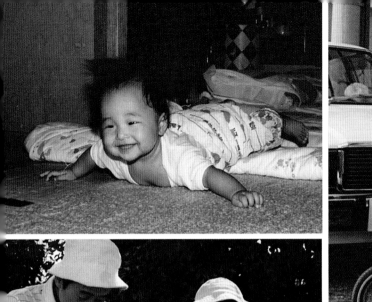

of place, and I still find that I'm learning new skills from her, such as what herbs to collect, how to prepare them, preserving techniques – many tips and tricks that you can't learn from a book but only by word-of-mouth. Unbelievably valuable. I hope I can leave my knowledge to our next generation!

MY LITTLE BABIES – LOVE AND MOMO

For those of you who love animals, you will understand that you can spoil your pets like you would your own child. We do so with our miniature collies, Love and Momo (which means 'peach' in Japanese). At the time of writing, they are 17 and 15 years old, and living with my parents. We love them dearly and my husband often comments that we spoil them too much. To him, I say: Never!

When I arrived in New Zealand, I wasn't quite homesick ... that was the wrong word ... rather I was 'dog sick'. I miss them so much and often want to return home just to see them and hug them. They are part of my family – and thanks to modern technology, nowadays I can Skype my parents and am able to see the dogs online. My brother does the same – he lives in a different prefecture from my parents and even he calls them over Skype just to see our babies.

My parents used to say that pets are good for teenagers and old people particularly – mainly because they keep good company!

MANNERS AND ETIQUETTE

親しき仲にも礼儀あり
SHITASHIKI NAKA-NI-MO REIGI ARI

Good manners even between friends.

Japanese are acclaimed throughout the world for their hospitality, politeness and attention to manners. I strongly recommend that you familiarise yourself with some basics before you travel to Japan or visit a Japanese home.

JAPANESE TABLE ETIQUETTE

Japanese etiquette and manners have been described in one simple rule: whatever you would do in the West, turn it on its head, do the complete opposite, and that will get you far in Japan.

SOME QUICK TIPS

1. Wait until everyone has sat down – don't just start eating first.

2. Top up other people's drinks before your own.

3. Eat what is given – it is customary to eat rice to the last grain, and being a picky eater is often frowned upon.

4. Before eating say 'Itadaki masu' (my husband was taught to pronounce this by saying 'eat a lucky mouse') and 'Gochisou sama' at the end of the meals to the host and/or restaurant staff when leaving.

AT HOME

Today more and more Japanese have developed the Western habit of eating at a dining table, but traditionally we still prefer to sit on the floor and eat at a lower-standing table. I have fond memories of our 'kotatsu', which is a low-standing table with a heater underneath the tabletop that is commonly used during the winter months. We also put a futon or duvet cover in between the floor and the tabletop so heat doesn't escape. I still remember I used to sleep with my friends around the communal kotatsu, keeping all our legs and feet warm underneath – often my dogs would be in there too. They are just like humans – they won't come out unless we are calling them for mealtime!

However, when traditionally sitting on the floor, we must sit properly with our knees down until we finished eating our meals – as kids, this was very painful until we became used to this. Only men are allowed to sit differently i.e. cross-legged – I always thought to myself, that isn't fair!

'ITADAKI MASU' + 'GOCHISOU SAMA'

At the beginning of a meal, we put both hands put together in front and say 'Itadaki masu' – literally meaning 'I humbly receive' or 'Bon appétit'. At the end of the meal, say 'Gochisou sama' ('It was a feast'), again putting two palms together in front of you – this is to show your appreciation of the meal to your host/hostess.

NOODLES

If you slurp when you eat noodles, don't worry or be shy! This demonstrates your enjoyment and acknowledges the tastiness of the noodle soup.

'OMOTENASHI NO KOKORO'

'Omotenashi no kokoro' translates to 'Having the warm heart to welcome your guests'. Since I was little, this term has been repeated to me over and over again – my parents were never strict about studying, but their discipline manifested in the manners my brother and I had to demonstrate when welcoming any and every guest who came to our home. As my mum ran a little party-planning business, we often had quite a few people who would regularly visit our home every day and night for meetings. My parents drilled into me the proper etiquette of how to greet, start small talk, offer little snacks and beverages such as green tea – all the elements of being a top hostess's assistant!

Omotenashi, however, doesn't mean that you have to spend a lot of money or be extravagant in any way to welcome guests. It actually refers more to the attitude or spirit of welcoming and hospitality. For example, you always cook using the best ingredients that you have in your pantry, and make the best effort to make guests feel totally comfortable and as if they are at their own home. It's very interesting; people will let their guard down and be extremely relaxed simply by being served a very nice cup of home-brewed coffee. Omotenashi is shown and judged by how you do things, and not what you have.

FOOTWEAR AT HOME

In Japan, it is considered an honour to be invited to somebody's home. Many Japanese regard their home as being too humble to entertain guests. Shoes are not to be worn inside – the floor level is often built to be higher than the ground or entrance level, as Japanese don't want their floor to be stained by any soil, sand or dust that may be attached to the soles of one's footwear. Instead, shoes are removed in the genkan (mudroom or entrance foyer), and often replaced with slippers. Genkan are found even in the small matchbox apartments that urban Japan has become well-known for, but they are often proportional to the apartment size – or, in other words, tiny! Just wearing socks is also acceptable in informal situations; however, they are not generally removed – bare feet is acceptable when visiting a close friend, but not otherwise. Similarly to the slippers that you may wear when entering a home, there are also separate slippers used when using a bathroom for reasons of hygiene.

Wooden geta are a form of traditional Japanese footwear that resemble both clogs and flip-flops. They are a kind of sandal with an elevated wooden base to keep the foot well above the ground. The difference in design to Western flip-flops is to avoid flipping dirt or water up the back of the legs, ensuring cleanliness. It is generally considered polite to wear shoes instead of sandals, but sandal-wearers may carry a separate pair of white socks to put over their bare feet or stockings, so that their bare feet will not touch the slippers that the host offers.

Photo by iStock

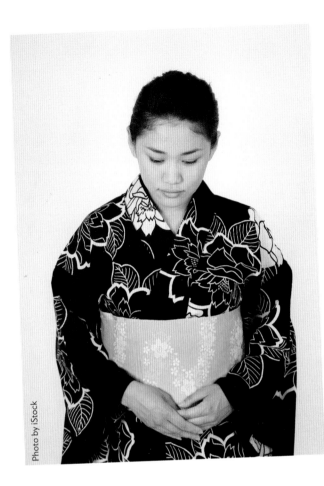

Photo by iStock

The first time I went back to Japan after living in New Zealand for a good two years, I hugged my parents and shook my aunty's hand – they immediately froze, as it is not our custom.

Japanese children learn how to bow from a very young age, but still to this day Japanese companies commonly provide training to their employees in how to execute bows. It is essential to know how to bow correctly if you want to conduct business in Japan.

Some bowing basics: keep your back straight and bow from your waist. For boys and men, hands should be on your side; for girls and women, hands should be clasped in front.

For business meetings we bow when we greet people on arrival and also on departure. Bowing is also essential when attending traditional ceremonies such as weddings and funerals.

Some people find it funny that we habitually bow even when we talk on the phone. If we receive a call from a customer or a person of superior position, you will see us bowing during the conversation. I have been in New Zealand for 16 years but I still have this custom and bow over the phone without noticing it, much to my husband's amusement.

A funny family story is the first time my husband came with me to Japan, we had had a few drinks and he forgot his etiquette – we'd been talking about the wedding dances we'd been practising, and my husband picked up my aunty and took her on a little pirouette. She had to sit down because of heart palpitations, as it was the first time in 30 years a man other than her husband had touched her!

Hopefully some of these tips help you to avoid any etiquette faux pas the next time you visit a Japanese home!

After entering a host's home it is important also that, after removing one's shoes, they are turned around so that the toes face the door for ease of re-putting them on. During the winter or if the day is especially cold, if a guest is wearing a coat or hat, the guest will remove the coat or hat before the host opens the door. When the guest is leaving, he or she does not put on the coat or hat until the door has closed.

BOWING

Bowing is one of the most iconic features of Japanese etiquette; it is part of my heritage. In Western culture, it is commonplace to shake hands, kiss cheeks and give hugs. In Japan, we hardly ever have physical contact with another person (apart from our spouses and children) – instead, we bow to each other to show respect.

WEDDINGS

Traditional weddings in Japan are absolutely beautiful. I went back to Japan a couple of years ago to attend my best girlfriend Sachiko's wedding.

Traditionally one wears a kimono during the ceremony (which typically lasts about 30 to 40 minutes), and then the bride and groom change to Western wedding dresses and suits for the reception, which is called 'kekkon hiroen' (and goes for about two and a half hours).

Just like many weddings, it was a celebration of a new couple as well as of the reunion of friends, and one of the highlights was the food. The newlywed couple chose a traditional Japanese menu and this was a seven-course feast. I normally never leave anything behind, but I couldn't finish the meals that night!

My husband and I were married in New Zealand, but we took wedding photos wearing kimonos in Japan. During the photo shoot you may notice I am dressed in different outfits and have different headpieces. Traditionally the bride wears pure white to declare one's maiden status to the gods. There are two types of headpieces: one, the 'watabōshi', is a white hood; the other, called the 'tsunokakushi', serves to hide the bride's 'horns of jealousy'. It also symbolises the bride's intention to become a gentle and obedient wife.

My husband wore a traditional montsuki (black formal kimono), haori (kimono jacket), and hakama (kimono pants). He found it very interesting and chose to break with tradition by smiling during a number of the photographs, which frustrated my mother no end!

I can't describe the sense of pride that I felt to wear a kimono which represents who I am on the most special day of my life.

JAPANESE FESTIVALS

14 FEBRUARY

バレンタイン VALENTINE'S DAY

In Japanese culture, on Valentine's Day, it is actually girls who are the proactive ones – they are the ones who give chocolates and profess their love to the boys. When I was at school, every male teacher and boy in the school would become extremely sensitive around this time, waiting to see how many chocolates they were going to get from girls! Shopping centres and supermarkets consequently would promote chocolate sales extensively around this season.

I remember that I used to bake a chocolate cake for my boyfriend, and would buy normal chocolates for my dad and my brother and they would complain and ask why they didn't receive the same love from me ...

There is also the term 'Giri-choko'; 'giri' means 'obligation' and 'choko' means 'chocolate'. Some office ladies give 'Obligation chocolate' to their co-workers, but unfortunately for the male ego it doesn't mean anything.

My dad used to come home with a bag of chocolate every Valentine's Day and my brother and I would eat them all for him! The trouble was he had to return the favour. We call this 'White Day' – when the man normally buys biscuits reciprocally for those who gave the chocolates to him in the first instance!

3 MARCH

雛祭り HINAMATSURI (GIRLS' DAY)

Hinamatsuri, also called 'Momo no sekku' (Peach Festival), is held on 3 March every year and is known as 'Girls' Day', where we celebrate the growth and long-lasting happiness of girls. Families with girls will often celebrate by displaying Hina-ningyou, which are tiered platforms covered with red carpet upon which stand beautiful Japanese dolls.

On Girls' Day we often eat chirashi sushi (you will find this recipe on page 128) and serve shiro sake, which is clouded sake. Special drinks and snacks are available in stores around this time, such as amazake (a sweet, non-alcoholic drink made from rice and koji mould), hishimochi (diamond-shaped rice cakes), and hina-arare (bite-sized

All photos courtesy of Sachie Nomura

roasted rice cakes) – these are my favourite sweets!

5 MAY

子供の日 CHILDREN'S (BOYS') DAY

This is a national public holiday when boys are celebrated. We wish for their happiness and that they grow up healthy. Often you will see carp-like steamers (called 'koinobori') made of cloth outside of houses (carps symbolise strength and overcoming future obstacles to become successful) and miniature samurai helmets, with armour and bows and arrows inside them. I still remember having the traditional sweet during our kyushoku (school lunch) called 'chimaki', which is a sweet rice cake wrapped in bamboo leaves.

7 JULY

七夕 TANABATA

Tanabata is also known as the Star Festival, and there is a story behind this date. We are told that two lovers, Orihime and Hikoboshi, were separated and only allowed to meet one day a year. On that day, 7 July, they can see each other through the Milky Way.

OCTOBER

お祭り FESTIVAL SEASON CELEBRATING HARVESTING OF FOODS

Each and every region will have their own special date for a festival to celebrate the harvesting season. We walk around the whole town carrying omikoshi, a portable Shinto shrine for the gods and spirits. It resembles a small building which is fixed to four poles. Omikoshi are usually very heavy and require many folk to carry it on their shoulders. There are a lot of hawker foods for sale, such as takoyaki, yakisoba, BBQ corn, sweets, roasted chestnuts and many more!

Particularly in our region, the Aichi prefecture, we have a special tradition called 'Mochi Nage' – meaning 'to throw away rice cake'. People gather all around the community, to both collect rice balls and throw them from roofs! Some other regions have different traditions, but this is our way to thank the heavens for the bounty that we have received for the year – I think.

Photos courtesy of Sachie Nomura

ARRIVING IN NEW ZEALAND

THE DIFFERENCE IN FOOD CULTURE

When I first arrived in New Zealand, I was 18 years old and full of curiosity. New Zealand also served to be the first overseas country I had ever visited and so everything to me was exciting – even pulling a string to stop the bus so I could jump out and compare the size of vegetables on a roadside stall. I will never forget the first time I went to the supermarket – I was gobsmacked to see the size of the capsicums! Huge!

WHAT DO JAPANESE EAT FOR BREAKFAST?

Many people often wonder what Japanese eat for breakfast. Unlike many Western breakfasts, we place importance on having a full meal – my traditional family breakfast consists of a bowl of white rice and miso soup. As sides we have grilled fish, egg rolls, nori sheets with some pickles, and sometimes small sausages. Nowadays many Japanese will simply have toast and coffee, but I love eating a full breakfast in the morning as it gives me the energy to work throughout the day. When my husband (who is part-Malaysian and part-Chinese) first visited Japan with me and had his first breakfast experience, his first response was 'Is this for dinner?' We all laughed and said, 'No, this is just for breakfast!'

In the region where I was born, in Hekinan city, there is an interesting morning habit ... we call it literally 'Morning!' It's when girlfriends will all get together and all trot to a café for breakfast. I have found in New Zealand, there are many lunch specials to attract customers through the doors, but in Hekinan our 'mornings' were fantastic value – normally you pay ¥500 (NZ$7.50) and it comes with toast, coffee, salad, egg, etc., but some places will also provide full Japanese meals for ¥500. When I came to New Zealand, I couldn't find anywhere that had the kind of value that I was accustomed to, so we often go to a local hotel instead, which is wonderful – but it hurts the pocket a lot more!

LUNCH BOXES

One thing that did shock me when I arrived was the state of lunch boxes that I saw Kiwi adults and children being served and eating. I see so much processed food, like chips and tasteless sandwiches laden with sugary spreads, which no doubt has an effect on children's concentration and development.

In most places in Japan, for children aged between 7 and 12 (and in some places to 15), the government subsidises and provides hot lunches (called 'kyushoku') cooked every morning and delivered to our schools. As children we have to learn how to work in a team and appreciate the importance of food, so we wear aprons, sanitary hats and masks and serve the meals to classmates. It's just like how kids in New Zealand volunteer to do traffic patrol and stop cars at pedestrian crossings outside schools.

I have wonderful memories of it, as the menu only repeated itself every four to six months and lunch was always a balanced full meal – a main dish with a couple of side dishes and milk, and even dessert for some special occasions. The meals were designed by nutritionists to be optimal for development, but they were extraordinarily tasty as well, so that as children we would want to finish everything! It had the added benefit of helping us learn manners around meals and to treat the occasion as a social one so you could enjoy lunch with your friends.

Consequently, I LOVE kyushoku meals! And it has become a huge passion of mine. It is a social change that I want to enact before I leave this Earth and hopefully we can make a change in the lunch box culture of Westerners.

Between the ages of 15 and 18, I had a daily lunch box prepared by me and mum. In Japan, we are

Photo by iStock

famous for bento – or boxed meals (although this label does not do it justice). Bento is very common and constitutes an important ritual during lunch. The ideas behind them are perfect nutritional balance, moderation, presentation and pride. The preparation of these meals begins the moment children finish kyushoku and Japanese mums take special care when preparing meals for their children. There are often 'bento-offs' where the mothers almost 'show off' their accomplishment in making lunch – it is almost a competition to see who is the best mother!

This may sound difficult to the time-bound person, but it all comes down to planning your meals well. You can cook slightly more dinner and leave some for the lunch box the next day – for example, we would make dumplings or spring rolls and freeze them so you only need to defrost and deep-fry them in the morning (no preparation required). Traditionally, bento boxes call for a 4:3:2:1 ratio of starch (rice or noodles or a staple), which staves off hunger; 'okazu' or side dishes comprised of protein (meat/tofu); fruits and vegetables; and desserts or condiments. This is not to be seen as an iron rule, but it does promote healthy eating and makes sure the meal is balanced and filling.

One of the main points about bento boxes is that 'the eye also eats' – meaning that apart from being nourishing, the food should also be attractive visually. You will often see incredibly artful presentations where a leaf may be cut out of an egg roll or an orange is made into the shape of a flower – and many more creative ways of presenting food to entice the eater to devour! Having said all of this, bento are sometimes made fancy, but the heart of the matter is that 'it must be consumed in its entirety'.

Of course, those people who can't make their lunch in the morning, eat out. My favourite foods to eat for lunch are ramen noodles, udon noodles, Japanese curry dishes and pasta too! One misconception is that bento has to be Japanese food – not at all! You can put anything you want into your box – it's more the principle and philosophy behind the importance of lunches that makes it a bento. These days different lunch boxes with compartments, heated thermal flasks and individual foil containers to keep foods separate and prevent sogginess are readily available thanks to the globalised world we live in. One favourite hobby of mine in Japan is to go to a shopping centre and buy new lunch items. You can easily spend a good couple of hours there!

With a bit more education on bento boxes and using seasonal ingredients, and by showing that it doesn't take that much extra time, we can start a Western Bento Revolution!

MEETING MY HUSBAND AND COOKING FOR A FAMILY

When I first started living with my husband, the first thing that he surprised me with was his diet – the foods that he was (or, in his case, was not!) eating. He ate only four dishes per week that we would rotate. If I can remember, they were oats and water; fish ball noodle soup; Singapore fried rice noodle; and old salad greens he would douse with vinaigrette and have with the discounted chicken from the supermarket at the end of the day. I guess food was not his first priority. When I moved into his place and cooked dinner on the first day, his response was 'Oh, are we celebrating something?' Having three or four dishes on the table was a 'celebration' for him, but it was very normal to me. Now we have at least three or four different dishes every night – that's how I grew up, so it wasn't hard for me to repeat the habit. However, the irony is that now he has been 'spoilt' and has these same high expectations everywhere we go – he won't even drink 'green-bottled' beer or 'non-reserve' wine anymore!

Also another very interesting habit that I noticed was that now when my husband eats poor food, his mood changes dramatically and he gets very grumpy. However, if he comes back home stressed out about whatever it is that is bugging him, and I feed him a nice home-cooked meal, his mood instantly changes.

You are what you eat – I agree!

梅はその日の難逃れ。
UME-WA SONO HI-NO NAN NOGARE

One Japanese plum a day is an escape from that one day's struggle

DON'T COOK WHEN YOU ARE ANGRY OR IN A BAD MOOD

When I was a child, I learnt that love transfers from your heart to your fingertips, to the foods that you touch. I recall being at an event as a young girl and helping my mum and relatives to make some lunch for 40 to 50 people. My aunties were all preparing a dish, and one of them was asked to finish up and plate the dish. All she did was mix the ingredients with her hands. She let me taste the dish before she touched it, and then immediately afterwards. I was shocked by how much the taste changed and in my adolescent mind was thinking, 'Wow – she has magic hands!' Later on, when I asked her why the foods tasted different, her answer was simply love from her hand – it is the secret ingredient.

When you care about people and cook food with love, it will transfer from your hand to the food and give it that something magical.

Someone sent me this quote once:

'Food is one part, and love is another part. Food will give people physical nutrition. Love and affection which you show will give people mental nutrition.' – Narayanan Krishnan

I have never forgotten it.

MY HUSBAND, THE SEAWEED EATER

There are a number of different types of seaweed in Japan and we love all of them – nori, wakame, konbu, etc. We use different types of seaweed for different types of dishes, such as miso soup, salads, stocks and garnishes. Another radical change that happened in my husband's diet after we met has been his substitution of dried seaweed sheets for chips as his choice of snack food!

I read somewhere recently that 69 per cent of Kiwis munched on potato chips in the last three months. I'm sure that's also more than just one serving or one bag. Needless to say that's A LOT of potato and a lot of chips!

I must admit that we also enjoy the company of a bag of chips now and again as a treat – particularly when there is a movie involved! However, we normally eat edamame beans or ajitsuke nori instead. It's very low in calories – only 4 calories per sheet. Also this seaweed is said to contain the same amount of protein as soybeans. These are quality proteins, and almost 70 per cent of it is easily digested by the human intestines. Nori is sometimes considered a superfood and is a reservoir of vitamins, such as vitamins A, B1, B2, C and iron.

Add that to the fact that just a couple of little packets takes away all the cravings, which means it's healthy on your wallet as well as the waistline!

起きて半畳 寝て一畳

OKITE HANJOU,
NETE ICHIJOU

*Meaning: You need just half a tatami mat
when awake, one tatami mat when asleep.
(That is, you need not be rich to live a
satisfied life.)*

SNACKS, SWEETS AND DRINKS

We Japanese aren't known for our large consumption of desserts, but what we do make we really appreciate. 'Oyatsu-time' is afternoon tea-time, when, at around 3pm, we savour delicate sweet treats such as green tea cheesecake.

My personal favourite sweet thing is my own creation: my miso walnut brownie. Inspiration for this came when I was visiting the 200-year-old miso factory in Nagano. I hope you enjoy the recipe as much as my family and I do.

ライチカクテル

SAKE LYCHEE COCKTAIL

SERVES
4

PREPARATION TIME
15–20 minutes

COOKING TIME
nil

INGREDIENTS

1 orange

565g tin lychees

120ml sake (do not use
  cooking sake)

2 egg whites, optional

3–4 handfuls of ice cubes

I just love the style of this cocktail – milky pink sophistication in a martini glass. The citrus oil from the orange will give you a lift when you taste the first notes on your tongue, but it's not overwhelming. If you include the egg white, it will create a white foam that sits on top of the drink. Please be sure to use a very fresh egg if you decide to do this.

METHOD

Remove half the orange peel with a paring knife. Keep peel in an airtight container in the fridge until needed. If you like, segment the orange and freeze the segments too.

Drain syrup from lychees and blitz fruit in a food processor. Transfer fruit to a colander over a bowl and squeeze out as much juice as possible. You should have about 200ml lychee juice in the bowl.

Put sake, lychee juice, egg white, if using, and ice in a cocktail shaker or jar and shake well for 15 seconds. Pour into a cocktail glass and squeeze in the oil from the orange peel. Add orange segments if you have them.

モヒート

GEISHA'S MOJITO

SERVES
1

PREPARATION TIME
3 minutes

COOKING TIME
nil

INGREDIENTS
handful of mint leaves
½ lime, cut into 4 wedges
ice cubes plus a couple
 extra to serve
2 oz (60ml) sake (do not
 use cooking sake)
1 oz (30ml) blackcurrant
 fruit cordial
½ cup (125ml) soda or tonic
 water

This is a great drink for when the taste of sake is new or a bit unfamiliar to you – or even as a different way to enjoy your sake at home.

METHOD
Put mint leaves in a glass and squeeze in 2 of the lime wedges. Use muddler to bruise mint and release flavour.

Fill glass with ice and add sake and blackcurrant cordial.

Top up with soda or tonic water and stir well.

Add a couple more ice cubes and lime wedges to serve.

蓮根チップス

RENKON CHIPS

SERVES
2–3

PREPARATION TIME
5 minutes

COOKING TIME
20 minutes

INGREDIENTS
1 tsp vinegar
2 frozen lotus roots
  (renkon), defrosted and
  finely sliced
canola oil, for deep-frying

SEASONING
1 tsp sea salt
¼ tsp chilli flakes
zest of ½ lime

Anyone who loves potato chips must try renkon chips. Renkon is a lotus root with a unique texture. Enjoy with the seasoning mix on top to add flavour. Perfect with a beer!

METHOD

Preheat oven to 180°C. Stir vinegar into 1 litre cold water.

Soak lotus root in vinegar water for 2 minutes to avoid discoloration. Pat dry with paper towel and place on a paper-lined baking tray.

Bake for 15–20 minutes to dehydrate the lotus root (this will make the chips crispy later on).

Heat oil in a small pan or wok to 180°C and deep-fry lotus root for 1 minute or until light golden.

Meanwhile, to make seasoning, mix together all ingredients.

Drain chips on paper towel and sprinkle with seasoning while still hot. Store in an airtight container for up to a few days.

唐揚げ
DEEP-FRIED CHICKEN
'KARAAGE'

Everybody loves deep-fried chicken – well, I do! And, this may create some heated debate, but I do think the Japanese make the best fried chicken. Tender, juicy and delicious, karaage taste great even when cold, so take them on picnics or pop them in your lunch box. I often have these with a little lemon juice or dipped into Japanese mayonnaise.

METHOD

Combine ginger, garlic, soy sauce and sake in a bowl.

Add chicken to marinade, mix well and leave in fridge for 20 minutes or more.

Heat oil in a pan or deep-fryer to 180°C.

Mix starch and flour together and coat chicken, dusting off any excess.

Lower a piece of chicken into hot oil. Deep-fry for 2–3 minutes until cooked through.

Drain on paper towel and serve with lemon, parsley and Japanese mayonnaise.

SERVES
4

PREPARATION TIME
25 minutes plus 20 minutes refrigeration

COOKING TIME
10 minutes

INGREDIENTS
600g boneless chicken thighs (about 4), cut into large bite-sized pieces
1 Tbsp grated ginger
1 Tbsp grated garlic
4 Tsbp soy sauce
2 Tbsp cooking sake
canola or rice bran oil, for deep-frying
½ cup potato starch or corn starch
½ cup plain flour

TO SERVE
lemon wedges
chopped parsley
Japanese mayonnaise

おし寿司

SUSHI CAKES

MAKES
22 bite-sized cakes

PREPARATION TIME
15 minutes

COOKING TIME
nil

INGREDIENTS

80g cold smoked salmon
  slices
3 cups cooked short- or
  medium-grain rice
2½ Tbsp sushi vinegar (use
  ready-made or see recipe
  on page 118)
2 Tbsp sushi ginger, finely
  chopped
1 Tbsp black sesame seeds
salmon roe or finely
  chopped capsicum, to
  garnish

Are you struggling to roll your own sushi? Good news –
you don't need a sushi mat to make these delightful little
cakes. You can use ramekins or be creative with muffin
tins, cake tins or any other small containers to make
different shapes.

METHOD

Line a small muffin tin with plastic wrap, letting the plastic hang over
the sides.

Place half a piece of smoked salmon inside each cup.

Mix cooked rice with sushi vinegar, ginger and sesame seeds.

Spoon rice on top of smoked salmon in the tin. Press gently and cover
with plastic wrap to prevent drying out. Set aside for 5 minutes.

Turn muffin tin upside down to remove sushi cakes. Remove plastic
wrap and garnish with salmon roe or capsicum.

ピザまん、あんまん
HOT SNACK BUNS

MAKES
8 buns

PREPARATION TIME
15 minutes plus 1 hour
resting the dough

COOKING TIME
10–15 minutes

INGREDIENTS

DOUGH
1 tsp dried yeast
2½ Tbsp white sugar
1 cups plain flour
⅓ cup glutinous rice flour
½ tsp flaky sea salt
1 tsp baking powder

SAVOURY FILLING
1 Tbsp oil (any type except
  olive oil)
chopped bacon or sausages,
  optional
¼ onion, sliced
2 mushrooms, sliced
1–2 Tbsp tomato pizza
  sauce
salt and black pepper, to
  taste

SWEET FILLING
red bean paste (anko)

I used to eat these hot buns on my way home from school in winter. They were filling on cold days and kept my belly warm! I use red bean paste or a pizza-like filling, but you can use anything. These buns freeze well – keep them in a zip-lock bag after steaming if you can't finish them all.

METHOD

Mix yeast and sugar with 150ml lukewarm water in a bowl and leave for 5 minutes.

Mix flour, glutinous rice flour, salt and baking powder in a large bowl and add yeast liquid. Mix well to form a dough.

Knead for 10 minutes or until dough is smooth. Cover with a wet cloth and leave for at least 1 hour until doubled in size. (If it's a cold day, warm the oven to 40°C and leave the bowl inside for an hour.)

For savoury filling, heat oil in a small frying pan over medium–high heat. Add bacon or sausage, if using, and fry for 1 minute. Add onion and mushroom and cook for another minute. Add pizza sauce, season with salt and pepper, mix well and set aside.

Divide dough into 8 pieces and flatten with rolling pin or your hand. Place savoury or sweet filling on middle of the dough and close dough over the top, as shown in pictures (see pages 210–211). Place each bun on a coaster-sized square of baking paper.

Steam buns for 10 minutes and serve hot.

1 2
3 4

海苔の佃煮

NORI AND SHIITAKE PASTE

MAKES
200g

PREPARATION TIME
5 minutes

COOKING TIME
15–20 minutes

INGREDIENTS

6 nori sheets, cut into small pieces
3 Tbsp soy sauce
3 Tbsp mirin
3 Tbsp cooking sake
1½ Tbsp brown sugar
3 medium-sized dried shiitake mushrooms, soaked in 300ml hot water for 10 minutes (save the soaking water) and finely chopped
toasted sesame seeds, to garnish

Have you ever wondered what you could do with oxidised nori sheets, other than throwing them away? This is a rescue remedy for creating a delicious seaweed paste that you can simply add to steamed rice or use as a stuffing for rice balls!

METHOD

Put all ingredients with 250ml shiitake stock in a saucepan over medium–high heat.

Bring to the boil, reduce heat to medium and simmer for 10–15 minutes until most of the liquid disappears and nori becomes a paste.

Store in an airtight container in fridge for up to a week.

Garnish with sesame seeds to serve.

醤油キャラメルのアイスクリーム

SOY CARAMEL ICE CREAM

When I visited the 150-year-old soy sauce factory in Tokyo, I was amazed to discover that there are 300 different flavours that can be identified in just one drop of soy sauce, such as mocha, vanilla, rose, coffee ...

When I came back to New Zealand, I experimented and this soy caramel sauce was born – it tastes similar to toffee, but with its own unique twist!

METHOD

To make soy caramel sauce, mix white chocolate, soy sauce and cream in a small stainless steel bowl, then place over a pan of gently simmering water. Stir constantly until consistency of smooth caramel. Remove from pan and leave to cool.

Pour soy caramel sauce over softened ice cream and mix gently. Pour into a shallow tray, cover and freeze for at least 2 hours.

Scatter with crushed walnuts, or serve with more soy caramel sauce if you like!

SERVES
4–6

PREPARATION TIME
10 minutes plus 2 hours setting

COOKING TIME
5 minutes

INGREDIENTS
1 litre vanilla ice cream, softened at room temperature
crushed walnuts, to serve

SOY CARAMEL SAUCE
150g white chocolate
2 Tbsp soy sauce
2 Tbsp cream

スイートポテト

JAPANESE SWEET POTATO BITES

MAKES
10 bite-sized pieces

PREPARATION TIME
10 minutes

COOKING TIME
15–20 minutes

INGREDIENTS
300g kumara, peeled
2–3 Tbsp sugar
1 Tbsp cream
15g butter
pinch of salt
1 egg yolk
pumpkin seeds or chopped
  pistachios

I used to be nicknamed Kumara Girl when I was a child as I love any sweet food made with kumara. My favourite is to simply wrap it in tin foil and throw it into a bonfire or on the barbecue. However, this recipe is slightly more sophisticated and is a lovely treat to have with your cup of tea or coffee. You might need to adjust the amount of sugar depending on the sweetness of your kumara.

METHOD
Preheat oven to 180°C.

Cut kumara into big bite-sized pieces and boil in plenty of water for about 8–10 minutes or until tender.

Drain, put kumara back in the pan and add sugar, cream, butter and a pinch of salt. Mash until smooth.

Scoop a dessertspoon of mash and use another spoon to scoop it off and pass back and forth between the spoons to form oval-shaped quenelles. Place kumara quenelles on a baking tray lined with baking paper.

Brush with egg yolk, sprinkle pumpkin seeds or pistachios on the top and bake for 7–8 minutes or until lightly golden.

抹茶のチーズケーキ

GREEN TEA CHEESECAKE

SERVES
8

PREPARATION TIME
30 minutes plus 2 hours
refrigeration

COOKING TIME
nil

INGREDIENTS
150g biscuits (I use malt
    biscuits), crushed
35g butter, melted
sesame seeds
250g cream cheese
60g sugar
2 Tbsp lemon juice
100g plain yoghurt
1 cup cream, whipped
3 Tbsp gelatine powder,
    dissolved in 50ml warm
    water
1 tsp matcha powder, plus
    ¼ tsp extra

We drink green tea all the time, at home or in restaurants, and it is an essential part of the Japanese culture. Matcha is a type of green tea often used in the formal tea ceremony, but it is also used in a number of Japanese desserts. It doesn't give a strong tea flavour but creates a nice colour and slight dry tartness at the end of the palate. This cake is very light and refreshing compared to many New York-style cheesecakes.

METHOD

Mix biscuits and butter and press into base of a 24 cm round cake tin. Spread evenly and press with the palm of your hand. Sprinkle with sesame seeds and refrigerate to firm up.

Mix together cream cheese, sugar, lemon juice and yoghurt until smooth. Mix in whipped cream. Add dissolved gelatine and mix very gently.

Pour half mixture into cake tin over biscuit base. Spread with a rubber spatula and return to fridge.

Mix matcha powder with 1 tablespoon water until smooth. Pour into remaining half of cheesecake filling and mix well. Pour gently into the tin, keeping 1 tablespoon of filling mixture to use for decoration. Use rubber spatula to spread and make a flat surface.

Add ¼ teaspoon extra matcha powder to the 1 tablespoon filling to darken it for decoration.

Use a teaspoon to draw lines on the cheesecake with the darker matcha mix. Use chopsticks to drag horizontal lines and make patterns, as shown in pictures (see page 220). Refrigerate for 2 hours before serving.

桃栗三年柿八年

MOMO KURI SAN NEN
KAKI HACHI NEN

Meaning: Planted peach and chestnuts seeds take three years to bear fruit, persimmons take eight.
(That is, it often takes time to bear the fruit of one's actions.)

味噌とくるみのブラウニー

MISO WALNUT
BROWNIES

SERVES
6–8

PREPARATION TIME
20 minutes

COOKING TIME
20 minutes

Ingredients
1 Tbsp white or mixed miso
1 Tbsp plain yoghurt
125g butter, softened
1 cup brown sugar
1 cup walnuts, coarsely
  crushed
1¼ cups self-raising flour,
  sifted
plain yoghurt or whipped
  cream, to serve

Most people are familiar with miso in savoury dishes such as soup or marinated fish, but have you ever thought of using miso in desserts? You'll be surprised at how it adds depth of flavour to sweet foods. I suspect it may soon become your secret ingredient!

METHOD
Preheat oven to 180°C. Line a 15 x 27cm loaf tin with baking paper.

Mix together miso and yoghurt.

Mix butter and brown sugar in a large bowl until smooth. Add miso/yoghurt and two-thirds of the walnuts and mix well.

Add flour and mix well.

Pour into cake tin and sprinkle with remaining walnuts. Bake for 20 minutes.

Cool in cake tin, then serve with yoghurt or whipped cream.

カボチャのモンブラン
PUMPKIN TARTS

To let you all into a family secret: if ever my father had an argument with my mum, he would buy cakes as an apology and peace-offering. Of course, my brother and I didn't know this, so we always enjoyed the little treats and asked for more (cakes, not arguments). These tarts were among his favourite offerings.

METHOD

Mix mascarpone cheese and icing sugar together, being careful not to overmix or it will curdle. Fold in whipped cream.

Spoon mixture into a piping bag and pipe into pastry cases with a circular motion to make little mountains of filling. Place in fridge for 3–5 minutes to set.

Mix cooked pumpkin in a food processor until smooth and paste-like. Transfer to a small saucepan and place over medium heat for a couple minutes until slightly thick. Set aside to cool down.

Spoon paste into a piping bag with a small nozzle. It's time to make pumpkin noodles …

Hold piping bag tight and squeeze pumpkin noodles on top of mascarpone filling. Move piping bag from side to side to cover the filling.

Garnish tarts with pistachio or pumpkin seeds. Refrigerate until ready to serve.

MAKES
8

PREPARATION TIME
20 minutes

COOKING TIME
10 minutes

INGREDIENTS

200g mascarpone cheese
50g icing sugar
100ml cream, whipped
8 sweet pastry tart cases
300g pumpkin, cooked until soft
pumpkin seeds or chopped pistachios, to garnish

胡麻ロールケーキ
SESAME SEED ROLL CAKE

SERVE
6–8

PREPARATION TIME
20 minutes plus 2 hours
refridgeration

COOKING TIME
30 minutes

INGREDIENTS
4 egg yolks
120g caster sugar
50ml grapeseed oil
50ml milk
35g black sesame seed
  powder
100g self-raising flour
5 egg whites

WHIPPED CREAM
350ml cream
50g caster sugar

I absolutely love the look of this roll cake – the way the black sesame seed sponge contrasts with the cream. The softness of the sponge is just delightful to taste. Use the freshest eggs here.

METHOD
Preheat oven to 160°C.

Beat egg yolks and half the caster sugar in a large bowl until smooth, light and fluffy. Add oil, milk and sesame seed powder and mix well.

Sift the flour into the batter and mix well.

In a separate bowl, whisk egg whites and remaining sugar until soft peaks form. Add one-third of egg white to mixture and mix well. Add another third and fold in gently with a rubber spatula. Add rest of egg white and fold in gently.

Line a 34 x 37cm tin with baking paper, pour in cake mixture and bake for 30 minutes or until a skewer poked into the cake comes out clean. Remove from tin to cool.

Meanwhile, whisk cream and sugar together in a large bowl until soft peaks form.

Place the cooled cake on a flat surface and spread the whipped cream evenly over the top. Roll up the cake to create a log, and cover with plastic wrap.

Rest in the fridge for at least 2 hours before serving.

小豆とオレンジのアイス
ORANGE AND RED BEAN
ICE CREAM

SERVES
2–3

PREPARATION TIME
20 minutes plus 3–4 hours
freezing

COOKING TIME
5 minutes

INGREDIENTS
3 egg yolks
30g sugar
100g red bean paste (anko)
zest of 1 orange
200ml cream

Many people use red beans in savoury dishes, but in Japan we use them in sweet food. The zest of the orange gives the ice cream a unique lift.

METHOD

Boil water in a small pan and then reduce heat to medium–high.

Put egg yolks and sugar in a small bowl and rest on top of the pan.

Mix egg yolks and sugar until smooth, fluffy and light yellow. Remove bowl from heat and add bean paste and orange zest. Mix well.

Add cream and whisk until mixture holds soft peaks.

Pour into a clean container and freeze for 3–4 hours. Ready to serve!

ビートルートの大福

BEETROOT MOCHI
WITH RED BEAN PASTE [DAIFUKU]

MAKES
8 small mochi

PREPARATION TIME
15 minutes

COOKING TIME
nil

INGREDIENTS
160g red bean paste (anko)

DOUGH
100g glutinous rice flour
2 tsp caster sugar
1 tsp grated beetroot
2 Tbsp glutinous rice flour
  or potato starch, for
  dusting

Japanese rice cakes (mochi) are made with glutinous rice. This particular recipe is one of the most famous mochi desserts and is called 'daifuku' – 'dai' meaning 'big' and 'fuku' meaning 'luck'. It has a delightfully sweet filling that is sure to captivate you on your first bite. I use beetroot to provide a lovely pink colour and a subconsciously earthy taste. And I use ready-made red bean paste to save time. I wish you great luck while you're making your 'big luck' mochi! I serve these with hot green tea.

METHOD

Divide red bean paste into 8 portions and roll into nice round balls. Place on a tray and keep in the fridge.

Mix glutinous rice flour and caster sugar together in a bowl and set aside.

Stir grated beetroot into 120ml water to extract colour.

Place a colander on top of bowl of flour and pour in beetroot water.

Mix well until there are no lumps and then microwave for 1 minute on high. Mix dough with a wet spoon and microwave for another 1 minute on high or until dough is cooked through (dough will become translucent).

Now you have to move quickly! Dust work surface with glutinous rice or potato starch and quickly put dough on top of flour. Dust a little more glutinous rice flour on top of dough to make it easier to work.

Divide dough into 8 portions with a knife and flatten each one with your hand. Wrap around the balls of red bean paste and close the gap by pinching the ends together.

Place dough balls back on work surface, hold gently with your hand and move anti-clockwise to make round.

大学芋
'DAIGAKU IMO'
UNIVERSITY POTATO

This sweet treat reminds me of university and days spent studying without much money ... The solution? University potato: a cheap and simple but delicious dessert. To make this extra-special, serve on top of deep-fried strips of filo pastry.

METHOD

Cut kumara into chunks slightly bigger than bite-size and soak in water for a couple of minutes.

Drain and pat kumara with paper towel to remove any excess moisture.

Heat oil in a small pan and deep-fry kumara for 2 minutes or until cooked through. Drain on paper towel, place in a stainless steel bowl and set aside.

Meanwhile, put sugar and 4 tablespoons water in a small pan and bring to boil, caramelise (until it coats the back of the spoon), and remove from heat.

Drizzle hot caramel over kumara and toss to coat.

Sprinkle with toasted sesame seeds to serve.

SERVES
4

PREPARATION TIME
5 minutes

COOKING TIME
10 minutes

INGREDIENTS
2 kumara (300g each), unpeeled
canola oil, for deep-frying
90g coffee sugar crystals
2 tsp black or brown sesame seeds, toasted, to serve

胡麻アイス

HOME-MADE SESAME SEED
SEMIFREDDO

SERVES
2-3

PREPARATION TIME
15 minutes

FREEZING TIME
3-4 hours

INGREDIENTS
3 egg yolks
60g white sugar
3 Tbsp black sesame seed
  powder
200ml cream

I often hear from people that they think making ice cream from scratch is too hard, particularly with the plethora of ready-made options available. With this recipe, it will only take you 15 minutes to prepare and the rest of the work is done for you in the freezer! This black sesame seed ice cream is so simple to make and has an unique nutty texture and taste that I bet you will have never experienced before. It's sure to become an instant favourite!

METHOD

In a small-sized pot, bring water to the boil and then reduce the heat to medium-high so the water is simmering.

In a metal or heatproof bowl, add egg yolk and sugar and place over the simmering water, making sure the water doesn't touch the base of the bowl. Whisk the egg mixture until it becomes smooth, fluffy and has a light yellow colour (about 5-7 minutes if using an electric whisk).

Remove the bowl from the heat and add black sesame seed powder. Mix well.

Pour cream in the bowl and whisk with an electric mixer until the mixture holds soft peaks.

Pour the mixture into a clean container and keep in the freezer for 3-4 hours.

TRAVEL DIARY: SACHIE IN JAPAN

Courtesy of Top Shelf Productions

21ST MAY: DEPARTING FOR JAPAN!

Early morning, woke up, took a taxi to Auckland airport. Left my phone behind, so before the trip had even started I had lost the director and the cameraman ... Found them just before boarding the Air New Zealand plane bound for Narita, Tokyo, and an 11-hour flight.

Managed to get a whole row to myself and watched three movies and enjoyed the meals: a Japanese breakfast of salmon, steamed vegies and rice; and, later, a Japanese lunch of chicken with yuzu, buckwheat soba noodles and sushi.

Arrived Narita 4.15pm. First thing to organise was the rail pass and cell phone, amid a sea of people with black hair!

We took a 'limousine' (actually, a bus called a limousine) for the hour's journey to the Shinyokohama Prince Hotel.

We finally had dinner, at 9.30pm, in the nearby restaurant – ten don tempura served on top of rice, with beer and pickles!

22ND MAY: YAMASA SOY SAUCE

First day of shooting, expected mild spring weather – instead was raining, and freezing cold at 15 degrees ... brrr ... Our first destination, at 6.30am, was the Chiba prefecture, Choshi city. There is a saying in Japan: no-one is ever early or late – there is only one time, and that's on time! We caught the bullet train from Yokohama Station to Tokyo (a journey of about 20 minutes), carrying 20 kilograms of camera gear. It's very easy to get lost during the morning rush of Japanese going to work – not the best time to be travelling!

We then spent two hours on the Shinkansen (bullet train), which travels at 300 kilometres an hour, to get to Choshi, where we met with Mr Ikegami – a representative from Yamasa Soy Sauce – who was our escort for the whole day.

Yamasa produces the finest Japanese soy sauce, with something like 90 per cent of Japanese chefs in New Zealand preferring the Yamasa brand for their customers. The scale of production is enormous. The land area of the factory is about nine times the size of the Tokyo Dome, which

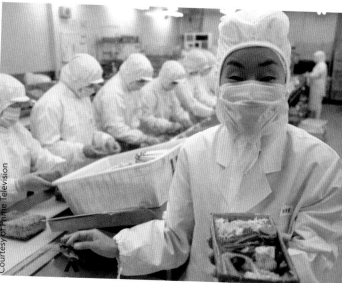

Courtesy of Prime Television

itself is 12 times the size of Auckland's Eden Park Stadium!

At the factory's entrance is a gigantic wooden barrel, over 100 years old, which was used for the process of making soy sauce – it is so large that you can stand inside.

Mr Kase, who toured us through, wasn't shy and explained the process of using soy beans, wheat, salt and koji, which is a mould over 360 years old – this determines the flavour and taste of the unique soy sauce. 'Moromi' is the process by which the soy sauce is fermented in tanks. There are hundreds of these tanks, with each tank making about 20,000 bottles. Wow, the room stank!

We then went to taste the house specialty, 'soy sauce soft ice cream', which is mocha-coloured and the first bite tastes of burnt coffee/caramel. Interestingly, soy sauce carries 300 different flavours and, as every person can interpret different flavours, it is apparently a fantastic ingredient when making sweet delights!

After the factory visit we had a sashimi lunch of tuna, red snapper and flounder, with braised fish.

Choshi city is close to the port and is renowned for the quality of its produce and also famous for its wet rice crackers. We headed to Inuboe Station (Dog Barking Station), and found two ladies sitting around a grill making the rice crackers, so we interviewed them. A cracker will take six to seven minutes to make, much like making a pancake, except during the heating process a wooden stamp has to be constantly imprinted onto the cracker to ensure the sides don't curl. When the morsel is browned, it's dipped into soy-based sauce, and voila! You have a delectable specialty of the region: wet rice cracker!

23RD MAY: BENTO BOX DAY!

In Japan we have many kinds of lunch boxes called 'ekiben' (station) lunch boxes. To begin the day we caught a train to Tokyo Station to meet Mr Izumi, who showed us the bento box factory, where we learnt how bento boxes are made, delivered and then procured by the various train stations in the mega-city. As you can imagine, hygiene was super-duper strict, just like in a nuclear power plant, with special shoes, hoses, clothes, everything!

The company runs 24 hours non-stop and is over 100 years old. Production lines have about 30 women per line – we were told only women are hired, because only females could be so precise and efficient for the job! Japanese kaizen efficiency – in the chilly 18-degree temperature adopted for sanitary purposes – was amazing to see.

A number to make your mind boggle: 40,000 lunch boxes are made daily for about 10 local train stations! Not only that, but imagine how many other stations exist outside of Tokyo! Interestingly, the best-seller in Tokyo is the chicken lunch box.

In the second half of our tour we visited the food-manufacturing areas of the factory. I had a lot of fun interviewing the executive chef as he explained the challenges of designing the menus. Colour and presentation is highly important in making the lunch box appetising. With 30 different ingredients in some lunch boxes, the challenge of creating ekiben versus meals served in a restaurant is that the bento box is served cold – even food that's meant to be served hot. There can be no compromise on taste or presentation.

The chef said there were three elements of etiquette that make the process of choosing the menus even more challenging:

- the food cannot have any sound – Japanese hate making noise, especially when in public, such as on the train (that's why you can't use cell phones in Japanese trains);

- the food cannot be too pungent, otherwise the smell when opening the lid might disturb fellow passengers; and

- the lunch box must be chopstick-friendly!

Ekiben is special to me because people in Japan will travel from station to station just like how we do in New Zealand with farmers' markets and wine tours! Each region has their own local produce and specialties, and I love the taste, colour and variety of every region's palate!

To get some sustenance we visited an udon noodle shop at the station. This Japanese 'fast food' is literally walk-in, walk-out – fresh udon is cooked within 1 minute 30 seconds. You can't compare the taste and healthiness with a burger alternative. Little wonder you don't see many overweight or obese Japanese.

The ekiben lunch boxes sell from around ¥800 to ¥3,500 (about NZ$10 to NZ$43). The selection process is made easy, with plastic replicas of each lunch box being on show. And each of the replicas displays the amount of calories, so from a deciding-what-is-best-for-my-weight point of view it is educational and informative amid a busy train station!

24TH MAY: RAMEN MUSEUM + CHINATOWN DAY

Today is Ramen Museum Day! With the crew we walked about 15 minutes to the Ramen Museum to meet Mr Takigami. From the outside the museum looks inconspicuous, but when you walk in you are instantly transported to a surreal world of circa 1958 Japanese streets! Just like *Back to the Future*, it was a time-warp. Even the ceiling was dark, to imitate a Japanese evening. Nine ramen shops lined the streets, celebrating the different regions of Japan and each of their

Courtesy of Prime Television

unique takes on the iconic national dish. We visited three restaurants, each highlighting soy-, pork- and miso-based soup stocks.

Soy is my preferred soup and, with 30 different ingredients used in the stock, the depth to the flavour was simply divine. The second restaurant celebrated the Kyushu taste (in the south) and declared that 100 per cent pork was used – and they meant it! The soup was milky, and the smell was – shall we say – unique, as only pork can be. The head, eyeballs, bones – everything was used in the soup. All I can remember is the pig head that was shown to me on a three-metre ladle by a worker who seemed terribly hung-over, perhaps from a bender the night before!

The third restaurant we visited sold miso-based soup from Hokkaido (in the north). They were incredibly protective of their recipe formulation. Unfortunately we weren't able to shoot the cooking, but we were able to taste. Very rich miso creaminess, and surprisingly unsalty. The noodles were very strong and chewy, to hold the broth. Definitely a cold-winter dish suitable for the climate in that part of Japan. Highly recommended.

We then embarked on a 40-minute train ride to Yokohama's Chinatown, full of colour, noise and, of course, people!

The first item we spotted was a steamed bun called 'nikuman', made by the winner of a world championship in steamed-bun making! Filled with pork mince, it was steamed in bamboo for seven minutes before arriving to the customer – the Asian version of a slider burger! We were lured in by a boy hawking with his placard: 'Come and try our bun, only ¥90 per bun!' This was the equivalent of NZ$1.50. How could we resist! And to differentiate their shop from the others, they had made the whole shop yellow.

The next shop was well-known for the size of their buns – they were the size of a double-fist, and centred with sweet-chilli prawns and pork kakuni (Japanese braised pork dish which literally means 'square simmered'). I tried the sweet sesame seed bun – beautiful but not recommended for eating when you are on a date, as you will end up looking as if you have black teeth like Jack Sparrow!

We decided to return to the Ramen museum for dinner and to catch up and have a drink with my cousin – all you can drink in 30 minutes for ¥500 (about NZ$6!) while being entertained by a guest yo-yo world champion competitor.

A great day, slept well.

25TH MAY: STATION FOOD

Woke up to a sunny morning! Did some shooting at the Tokyo platform of the new Shinkansen (bullet train).

Afterwards we ventured down to the shops at Tokyo Station. There were 32 premium food stores in one section. The first one we visited was a bakery shop, very famous for bread with red beans (anpan) – but specifically anpan that looks just like red bricks with the logo of Tokyo Station burnt into it. I managed to get into the tiny little kitchen.

Second was a Japanese sweet shop with mochi (rice cake) and Japanese jellies. However, the most interesting sweet was a soft-serve cone that was sandwiched in between CD-replica wafers. I recommend drinking something with it – it's very, very difficult to eat dry, as your lips will be stuck together as I found! There were also matcha (green tea) sweets, including a frozen matcha cheesecake.

There was also a kushiage (skewers) shop selling around 18 different types of skewers. Three or four people were making 2,000 or 3,000 skewers, in a space about a third the size of a small bedroom. The kushiage were mainly chicken-based, with a special dipping soy-sauce that had a secret recipe. I asked the chef to divulge the secret, and he said 'No!'

The final shop specialised in rice balls, with the number-one seller being a plain rice ball, lightly salted, so your palate can enjoy the quality of the grain of the rice without interference. I think I saw about 25 kinds of rice balls, some miso- or nori-based.

26TH MAY: TSUKIJI FISH MARKET

Woke up 2.30am to visit the largest fish market in the world – the Tsukiji market – 10,000 people are up even before me to get to work at this one location.

Our first destination was the tuna auction. It is very rare for a woman to be granted access to 'the man's world' – roughly about 150 tuna on the floor ready for auction, with seven or eight of them being from New Zealand (what I call 'All Black tuna!') – where I got told off for getting a little too close! The biggest tuna I spotted was 200kg from Italy!

Courtesy of Top Shelf Productions

The auction began at 5.30am, with some selling for US$20,000 per kilo! It was so vibrant and exciting to catch the energy of the auction live.

We then moved to the inner market to watch the filleting of the fish – the highlight was watching the use of a 1.5m Japanese steel knife, just like a *Kill Bill* Katana sword. The art of the cutting was to preserve the quality, and the precision was simply amazing. One thing we noticed is that there was no smell! Most people associate fish markets with smell and we were told that the fish was so fresh and of such high-grade that there was no stench. Lesson to all fish markets!

An old gentleman struck up a conversation with us – he had been working there for 50 years, and commented that he was a 'young person'! I managed to sample some of the tuna, with all varying levels of exquisiteness, much like how there are different cuts of beef – unbelievably rich in oil but just melts in your mouth, so you are left speechless.

The outer market contained a couple of restaurants for breakfast – it was already 8.30am and there was a queue of 40 people outside as everyone knows to come direct to the source for the freshest breakfast in the world. We found actual edamame plants, fresh wasabi and yuzu plums.

We were hungry for a bite with all this food, so stopped by a soba noodle station on the side of the road. Husband and wife combo. I ordered horse-mackerel tempura noodles, done within 30 seconds – the perfect fast food, and exactly what I needed.

27TH MAY: TRAVELLING + CURRY DAY

Travelling day from Tokyo to Nagano. Of course I had an ekiben lunch box – a balanced 30-item lunch box of 666 calories! Seasonal vegetables, rice, meat. Today we thought to fill our spiritual batteries by visiting a local temple to pray.

We found a tiny little curry establishment seating 16 – eggplant and mushroom curry with beer served in wine glasses! Salad, curry, soup and ice-cream, all for ¥1500 (around NZ$18.50).

Courtesy of Top Shelf Productions

28TH MAY: MISO DAY!

Left hotel 9.30am by taxi for the Marukome miso factory. We started the tour by watching a 15-minute video clip explaining the process, and then put on hygienic uniforms just like nuclear testers do! We proceeded to view the final bottling line – quite amazing that 120 packages of miso are packed each minute. What I found interesting is that, just like in the *Blues Brothers*, a lady sits in one spot and watches thousands of labels whiz by and checks the expiry date on every package. Quite amazing powers of concentration.

For lunch we visited a buckwheat noodle restaurant – very famous in Nagano. Cold buckwheat noodles, braised baby squid, rice balls in soup, steamed egg, and Japanese version of Turkish delight. Delicious but we couldn't finish it all.

In the afternoon we had a 45-minute drive into the mountains, to see Marukome's ancient Japanese warehouses (kura), where the premium miso is stored. Inside were 400 or so gigantic drums that store a tonne of miso – that's a LOT of miso! We were told that this miso was left to naturally ferment for four to five years. My enduring memory is the totally intoxicating fermentation smell. We used cucumber sticks to taste directly from the sauce – my original impression before trying was that it would be overwhelmingly salty, but it was incredibly surprising to me that the taste was sweet but had enough of a bite to use as an everyday dipping sauce. Perhaps this could be a new taste for Bluebird chips?!

On the miso was a brown liquefaction, which was explained by Mr Aoki as being the beginning of soy sauce.

Our next stop was for gelato by the temple in Nagano, where we met an expat Australian who had a well-known local café. The house specialty was a miso-caramel-walnut concoction. My first reaction was to have pre-judgements, but after my prior experience at the soy sauce factory I was prepared for a totally different sensory experience. Creamy, salty *and* sweet!

29TH MAY: TOYAMA + BBQ

In the early morning we waved goodbye to Nagano and departed for Toyama, on the west coast of Japan, where my family live. The scenery passing through Japan is quite mesmerising out in the open countryside.

10.30am: My father and uncle, who I hadn't seen for a good two years, welcomed us at the station, and we were promptly whisked to the sake house for a spot of 'relaxing'! We were greeted by Mr Hayashi, the head of an 18th-generation family of master sake brewers – his family's sake house has been trading since 1626! Unfortunately we couldn't see the production process as it is made between October and March (Japanese winter) – so we did the next best alternative, which was a premium sake tasting of seven or eight different varieties. Similar to wine, the top notes were fruity to dry, with some best as an aperitif, and some best as dessert. We also managed to sample 10-year-old sake. In contrast to wine, though, sake should be consumed within two to three years of production, with 15 degrees being the perfect temperature because the tongue can then taste all the flavours.

We then left the sake house bound for a traditional Japanese barbecue at home. While travelling we noticed junior high school students were in the rice fields planting seedlings so, the next minute, I was in the field planting my sustainable crop! Brrr, my feet were freezing!

Around 5pm preparation for the barbecue began while my mother and I prepped the food, cutting vegetables (onions, cabbage and wild mushrooms from the mountain behind the family home),

meat (beef and pork), local fish (snapper) and 'anger-fish' soup with bamboo shoots. The whole family started to arrive at the house and with any good barbecue comes beer! Japanese use a concrete cinder-block grill rather than a big Rinnai barbecue as many in New Zealand use – it's much more like the robata or famed yakitori grills. We love to start with beer, then onto sake and shochu till 1am (when out comes the whisky!).

30TH MAY: MOUNTAIN WILD HERB PICKING

4.30am: Wake-up to prepare for wild herb picking in the mountains. An interesting fact: we have to wear small bells to scare off the black bears, who are more troublesome and dangerous than humans. There are even bear police, who are busier than the local police that have to keep people in line! One time when my husband went for a run, he forgot his little bell and didn't come back for an hour – we spent the whole time worrying about his safety!

We picked udo (a Japanese wild herb) and

Courtesy of Sachie Nomura

Courtesy of Sachie Nomura

Courtesy of Sachie Nomura

bamboo shoots. The bamboo shoots are often only 10–15 centimetres long so you need an eagle-eye, and most of the time you are crawling on the ground to locate them – needless to say, this results in serious muscle pains and aches the next day for this delicacy. However, we were VERY lucky this season that they were out and it was absolutely worth it.

While prepping the herbs we cleaned the shoots and boiled the water for what we call 'bamboo sashimi'. The shoots are boiled for 20 minutes, then drained and peeled, and dipped into wasabi and soy sauce. Because the women do the work we are the only ones who get to sample this very rare treat.

31ST MAY: KYOTO

Woke up and headed to Nishiki market where the epitome of Japanese haute cuisine come to get their produce.

We went to a pickle shop, which had 70 different varieties, and had been in production for 70 years. Asazuke pickles are literally 'lightly marinated',

while another variety was furuzuke, meaning 'old picked' – sometimes over two to three years old!

The rice shop we frequented had over 20 different kinds of white rice and five different kinds of brown rice. The best-selling is koshi-hikari from Niigata, but the shop is also a strong supporter of the Kyoto region. Kyoto rice is sweeter and slightly stickier.

An extraordinary invitation presented itself on our trip – dinner at Hyotei, one of the world's finest three Michelin–starred restaurants. The owner, Mr Takahashi, is the 14th-generation chef to run the legendary kitchen and personally welcomed us with a seven-course meal which was created and plated uniquely for us.

Founded some four centuries ago by the Takahashi family, Hyotei still welcomes guests 16 generations later. The restaurant's origins stem from its humble beginnings as a teahouse where travellers could rest, refresh and prepare themselves before entering the hallowed Nanzen-ji Temple, just up the road.

Japanese culinary habits are still male-dominated, so it wasn't surprising to see 20 men all in the kitchen. So it was an unbelievable privilege to be invited into his kitchen and

to hold a hamogiri knife – imagine a giant machete. The cooks at Hyotei normally spend around a decade training in the kitchens, many of them living on-site, sort of like a commune obsessed with serving the finest food. In homage to tradition and dedication to high art, ingredients are delivered every morning in fresh quantities by suppliers – some of whom have been supplying Hyotei for generations. The restaurant's signature dish is a simple soft-boiled egg, accented with a drop of soy sauce. This is the essence of Hyotei – a perfectly cooked egg, with a yolk of indescribable texture and softness – untainted and immaculate. This is also the essence of Japanese cooking – without tampering, letting the very best of a country's produce do its work.

Mr Takahashi specially prepared for us a specific sea-eel dish. To give an idea, you must spend seven to eight years watching before you are actually granted the chance to make the dish hands-on as the skillset is incredible! Sea eel has a huge number of microscopic bones that need to be cut through, so it needs extraordinary concentration and care – and, not only that, you also need to not affect the skin, which is only 1mm thick!

OUR MENU

- Sweet plum – it takes four to five days to prepare a solitary plum. Needles placed in each plum absorb liquid and remove the acidity.

- Snapper sashimi – only 1.5–1.8 kilograms of a female snapper is used.

- 2–3mm nuts that look like mandarins! These are handpicked and marinated for over 18 years. The texture was pear-like and the taste incredible.

- Japanese ratatouille – seasonal vegetables cooked in a dashi stock and lightly seasoned.

- Seasonal vegies with Japanese paua (abalone).

- Sushi.

- Japanese dessert with matcha tea.

Takahashi's philosophy is that 'Simplicity is good' – to enjoy flavours raw is best, because as soon as you use heat, some of the flavour evaporates, so he is forever asking himself, 'How can I enhance flavour with heat as a minimum?' It can take 10–20 years to perfect a single dashi stock – this is the perfectionist spirit of Hyotei!

It was a NZ$460 meal, but worth every cent!

1ST JUNE:
TEA CEREMONY

Left hotel 9am bound for a well-known temple called Kiyo-mizu Temple. Shocked by the amount of students present as something like 150 schools visit per day!

Arrived at the 130-year-old teahouse. Wore a kimono before the ceremony. The tea ceremony room was tiny – complete with low ceiling – Sjaak our cameraman hit his head many times! The whole ceremony can take up to an entire day but we managed to do the 'short-version' = 1 hour. This is a very expensive hobby, as you have to wear a different kimono each season, and the average kimono is NZ$15,000 upwards!

2ND JUNE:
OSAKA

All prepped to travel on the bullet train to Osaka – capital of the famed okonomiyaki dish. The first restaurant we visited was Takojyo, which specialises in okonomiyaki, run by a spirited

mother-and-son duo. The thickness of the okonomiyaki was considerably more than what I was used to – about double the size of the normal pancake, but their secret sauce was to die for.

In the afternoon I had time to window-shop for Japanese kitchenwares before convening at a seven-storey building full of different eateries where we relaxed with a beer and NZ$3 yakisoba (fried noodles). This is quite the contrast to New Zealand where normally we're used to ground-floor eateries; instead in Japan it's commonplace to have three or four restaurants per floor ascending vertically rather than horizontally along the street, as space is a premium!

3RD JUNE:
SAKAI KNIVES

Our last day of shooting in Japan! I was especially looking forward to visiting Sakai city – famous for knife-making.

There is something alluring about Japanese steel, perhaps due to our rich history with the Samurai and also because it is the essential piece in every cook's arsenal. I was privileged to meet

Mr Shinoda, who is president of the Sakai-koji knife company, which has been operating over 280 years. He supplies knives to Ferran Adria of El Bulli fame – voted world's best restaurant five times!

Firstly we spent time with a blade specialist of 57 years (!) experience, who was one of the last 24 recognised and accredited Japanese craftsmen. Rather than be a part of mass-production he harks back to old times, and makes only 12 knives a day in front of a 1400°C furnace. No machinery is present, as he uses his eyes and sixth sense to see temperatures and know when the perfect time is to forge the steel.

I was very honoured to have my name carved into my own knife which is extremely rare to have happen, and it made me more aware of my responsibility to showcase the Japanese culture to Kiwis and the world.

To conclude the trip we headed to Dotonbori, an extremely well-known food city, where we gorged on crepes, takoyaki (octopus balls), okonomiyaki and gyoza (Japanese dumplings). 'Kuidaore' means 'eat till you drop' – otherwise known as major gluttony – and this is the catchphrase of the Osakaian. So we ate till 10pm on our final night as, it is true, Japan never sleeps!

Courtesy of Sachie Nomura

Courtesy of Prime Television

過ちては改むるに憚ること勿れ

AYAMACHITEWA ARATAMURUNI HABAKARU KOTO NAKARE

*Meaning: If you make a mistake,
don't hesitate to correct it.*

THANK YOU

I would like to say thank you to Top Shelf Productions – Laurie, Brian, Juanita, Catie, Sjaak and team – for discovering me, and for seeing the onscreen potential that I never knew I had. Also without them the connections would never have been made with the team from HarperCollins – Finlay, Matt, Vicki and others – to create this amazing book that allows me to share my joy for cooking and passion for Asian expression. Thanks also to Prime Television for the use of images from the 2013 television series *Sachie's Kitchen*, and to Japanese Lifestyle for the beautiful ceramics that appear throughout.

And thank you to my wonderful team of Ronan, Deepika and Fallyn – without them, their teamwork and laughter, Sachie's Kitchen wouldn't be where it is today.

I would like to dedicate this book to three people in my life: my mum and dad, and my husband. Having a supportive family makes all the difference in life, and without them I couldn't be who I am now and nor have created what we have now. Thank you.

TO MY MUM AND DAD

I am so grateful for their love and support in everything – where I am today is because of them. My dad has a saying, 'かわいい子には旅をさせ' (Kawaii koniha tabi wo sase), meaning 'If you love your kids, let them go on their journey.' That is, if you love your children, don't over-protect them by having them beside you all the time. Let them have a journey, make mistakes, and let them learn and gain the strength to live their lives strongly. This means that one day when the parents are gone, the child can stand on their own.

My dad often tells me that it was hard for him to let me come to New Zealand, but it was the best choice he made, as he is so proud to see me now standing on my own feet and living my life the way I designed it. My mum and dad were very understanding and open; they let me do what I love to do and I hope my TV show and book can make them proud to have me as their child.

Thank you, Mum and Dad! I hope I can be the same person to my own children one day.

TO MY HUSBAND

Nick was the first person to see something in me and believe in me. He kept me going when I was down and he pushed me forward to where we are now. It is amazing how powerful the words 'I believe in you' are. It was enough for me to look forward, to just dream big and take action. I hope I am able to be strong enough to pass those same words to people who need the same little push from behind. Thank you, Nick, for believing me and I love you.

INDEX

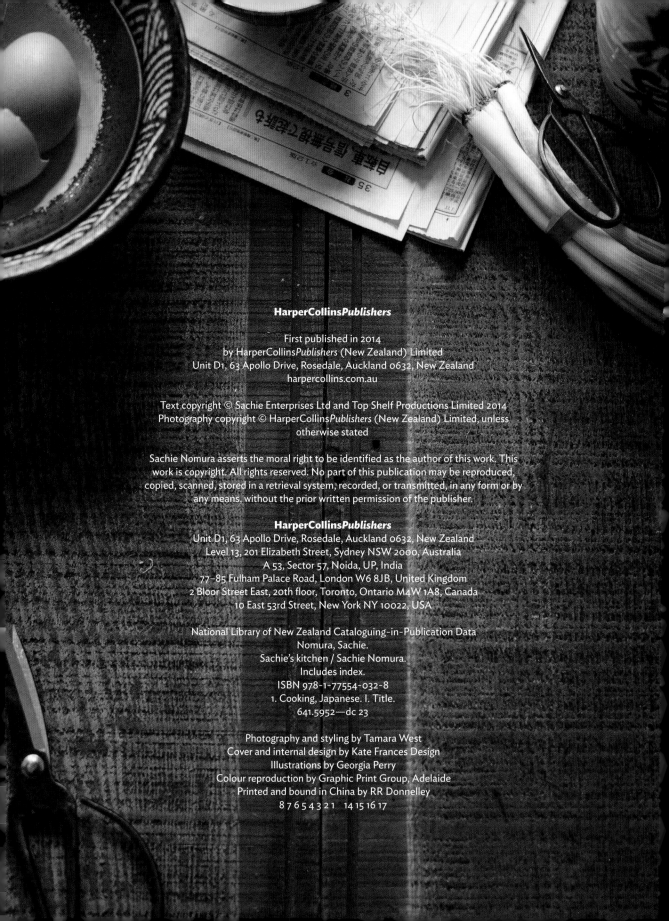

HarperCollins*Publishers*

First published in 2014
by HarperCollins*Publishers* (New Zealand) Limited
Unit D1, 63 Apollo Drive, Rosedale, Auckland 0632, New Zealand
harpercollins.com.au

HarperCollins*Publishers*

Unit D1, 63 Apollo Drive, Rosedale, Auckland 0632, New Zealand
Level 13, 201 Elizabeth Street, Sydney NSW 2000, Australia
A 53, Sector 57, Noida, UP, India
77–85 Fulham Palace Road, London W6 8JB, United Kingdom
2 Bloor Street East, 20th floor, Toronto, Ontario M4W 1A8, Canada
10 East 53rd Street, New York NY 10022, USA

National Library of New Zealand Cataloguing-in-Publication Data
Nomura, Sachie.
Sachie's kitchen / Sachie Nomura.
Includes index.
ISBN 978-1-77554-032-8
1. Cooking, Japanese. I. Title.
641.5952—dc 23

Photography and styling by Tamara West
Cover and internal design by Kate Frances Design
Illustrations by Georgia Perry
Colour reproduction by Graphic Print Group, Adelaide
Printed and bound in China by RR Donnelley
8 7 6 5 4 3 2 1   14 15 16 17